MW00617643

GET OUT ANY WAY YOU CAN

The Story of the Evacuation of House Seven

The CIA Propaganda Force in Vietnam

April 1975

Charles Eugene Taber

ISBN 0-7414-1583-6

Published by:

519 West Lancaster Avenue
Haverford, PA 19041-1413
Info@buybooksontheweb.com
www.buybooksontheweb.com
Toll-free (877) BUY BOOK
Local Phone (610) 520-2500
Fax (610) 519-0261

Printed in the United States of America

Printed on Recycled Paper

Published July 2003

For Lois, Sara, and Andrew

ACKNOWLEDGMENTS

The process of preparing this account of a challenging moment in my own, my own country's, and Vietnam's history, has renewed my gratitude to the many people who contributed to the positive outcome of this affair. First, I wish to express my respect for the fine work, patience, and bravery of my Vietnamese colleagues at House Seven. I wish also to thank my three American co-workers on Phu Quoc Island for the mutual assistance we offered one another. I must offer my sincerest gratitude to Captain Thien, Commander Tho, Lieutenant Dong, and the other Vietnamese military officials on Phu Quoc, who offered their help when under extreme stress of their own. It is essential that I thank Captain Boucher of The American Challenger for his humanity, shown in his willingness to take on board thousands of people in need. The marines on The American Challenger did an excellent job of maintaining order and keeping bellies full. The navy corpsmen provided expert medical care. Thanks are due also for the assistance offered by the Saigon Embassy.

Finally, and most of all, I must thank my wife Lois, whose love buoyed me all through this ordeal. My son, Andrew, carries on my love of adventure. My daughter, Sara, encouraged me to tell my story, and she, my son in-law, Peter, and grand-daughter, Maud, served as readers, and helped in essential ways during the final stage of the preparation of this manuscript.

VIETNAM

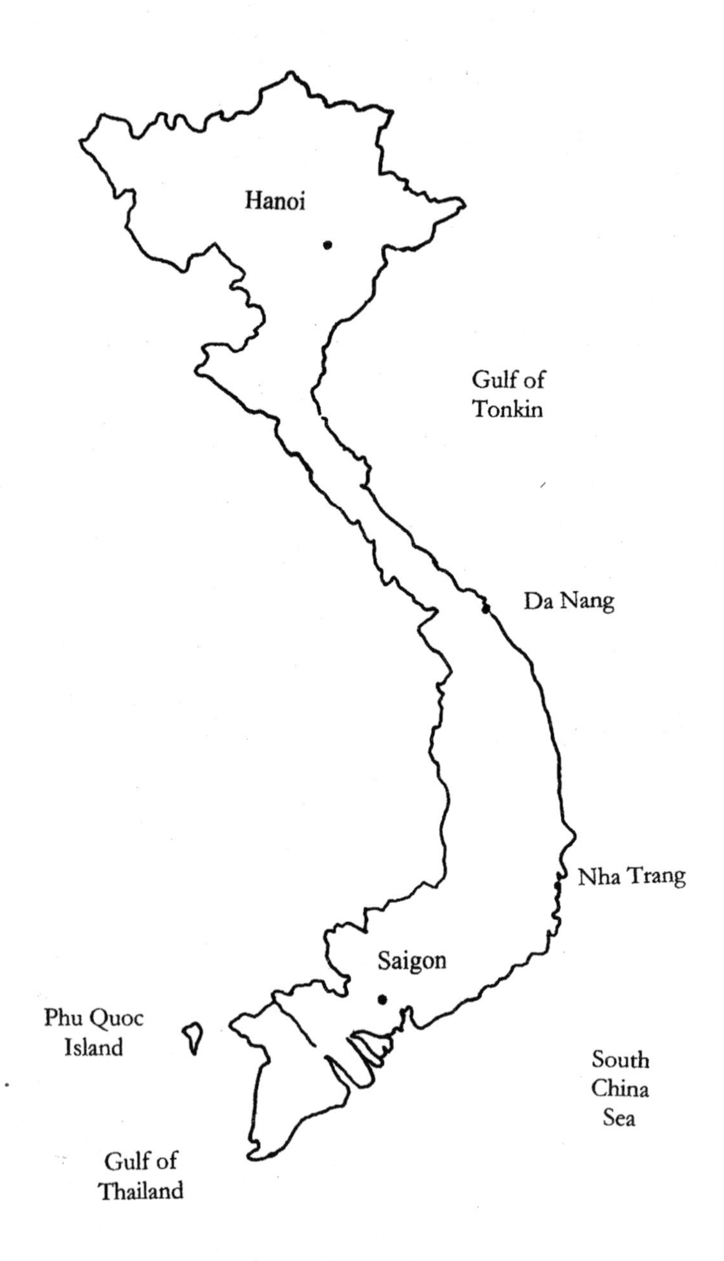
Hanoi
Gulf of
Tonkin
Da Nang
Nha Trang
Saigon
Phu Quoc
Island
South
China
Sea
Gulf of
Thailand

CONTENTS

PREFACE

Dear Mr. Ambassador:

I respectfully request that you give an order for the personnel of the Defense Attache's Office to leave Viet Nam within twenty-four hours beginning April 29, 1975, in order that the question of peace in Viet Nam can be settled early.

[Signed April 28, 1975 by Duong Van Minh, Interim President of the Government of South Vietnam]

In the early hours of April 30, 1975, I boarded a Vietnamese Navy landing craft pulled up on the sands of Phu Quoc Island. The vessel backed off the beach and headed out to sea--out of Vietnam's territorial waters. By the time the sun came up that morning, the Americans were out of Vietnam. Saigon's armed forces were unable to stop the armies of the north, the government capitulated and its American allies were ignominiously expelled from Vietnam. South Vietnam disappeared and a calamitous chapter in the diplomatic history of the United States came to a close.

Before the landing craft pulled itself off the beach, I led eight hundred Vietnamese employees of the CIA's Saigon Station aboard the vessel. The crowded craft--designed for 200 infantrymen--ferried me and the eight-hundred to the SS American Challenger, a United States Line freighter anchored about five miles offshore. Shortly after sunrise, three CIA colleagues and five hundred more Vietnamese employees boarded the ship from a second landing craft.

All safe on board, my colleagues and I congratulated ourselves--we had completed a task that only days before had seemed impossible. We had delivered over 1300 of our Vietnamese employees and their families from a fearful fate the conquering armies certainly intended for them.

The American Challenger remained anchored near Phu Quoc Island all day and took aboard more than two thousand frightened Vietnamese from a swarm of small boats which rowed, motored, or sailed out from the island throughout the afternoon and evening. They came in anything that would float, some half-full of water, several sank as soon as they reached the ship's ladder. Almost overloaded, ordered to leave Vietnamese waters, the Challenger sailed at midnight, the small boats still appealing to be taken, falling further and further behind.

The ship reached Agana, Guam six days later, and landed her human cargo safely into the refugee camps from which they would be set upon a course toward a new life in the United States.

My purpose here is to tell the story of how my three colleagues and I succeeded, in the chaos of war, in meeting a moral obligation to deliver our Vietnamese employees and their families to safety and, to give them a chance to rebuild their lives.

I am writing this story twenty-five years after the events, with only sparse contemporaneous notes to aid my memory. During the evacuation I recorded some events in a small pocket notebook, but I kept this to the minimum and in cryptic style, spies do not keep diaries. Helpful also was a long letter I wrote to my wife and children during the six days I was on the American Challenger. My memory of those events has been refreshed through the years when I have had occasions to relive the events with colleagues who were there.

I have changed the names of the CIA colleagues mentioned, some of whom still work for the Agency. Chief of Station Tom Polgar is so well-known that I left him his true name.

ASSIGNMENT VIETNAM

In the summer of 1973 I was on duty at the Central Intelligence Agency headquarters at Langley, Virginia. I was just a year returned to the States from my last foreign assignment (Tokyo) and was working as a desk officer guiding several covert propaganda operations designed to influence foreign governments to support US foreign policy objectives, among others, US policy toward Vietnam and the fragile cease fire which Secretary of State Henry Kissinger and Le Duc Tho had negotiated in January 1973.

Always eager to get back in the field, I had just about pinned down an assignment to London, when I got a call to the Far East Division front office. The executive officer told me Saigon Station had requested an experienced covert action officer soonest. "You are that officer," he said. I was not especially surprised. It had been accepted wisdom in the Vietnam War years that there were only two kinds of operations officers, those who had been there and those who were going to Vietnam. My turn had come. I was reluctant to serve in Vietnam. There was no fighting the assignment, I had to accept the job or get out. I still had five years to go before I could retire.

I arrived in Saigon on September 7, 1973. South Vietnam was at peace, albeit an uneasy peace. The cease fire agreement was holding in the main although there were frequent violations by both sides. The International Commission of Control and Supervision (ICCS), established under the agreement to enforce the cease fire, was ineffective. It was clear that Hanoi did not intend to let the agreement interfere seriously with its strategic goal, control of all of Vietnam. The Saigon government also violated the peace pact by moving into territory left to the communists by the agreement.

The Paris agreement required the United States to withdraw all fighting forces from South Vietnam and indeed we had pulled our combat troops out of the country. We left behind a small logistics force, the Defense Attache's Office, to manage the arms aid we continued to supply to the Saigon government. It was US policy also to provide political and intelligence support to the South Vietnamese government. CIA continued to play a role in Vietnam in support of the US mission.

In this era of imperfect peace I was to serve as an advisor to a propaganda radio project run jointly by CIA and the Psychological Warfare Command of the Army of South Vietnam (ARVN). The radio project had been set up in response to a request from National Security Advisor Henry Kissinger calling on CIA to take action to bolster the South Vietnamese in countering Hanoi's violations of the peace accords. Saigon Station and the Psywar Command had pulled together a staff of broadcasters and propagandists and set up a radio operation, three transmitters broadcasting in Vietnamese and two in Cambodian. The broadcasts were calculated to convince North Vietnamese and Vietcong troops to give up fighting and dying and accept the peace offered by the Paris Accords.

The most effective of the five radios broadcast under the legend "Mother Vietnam," represented itself as the voice of a patriotic third-force group, independent of both Saigon and Hanoi, seeking peace and democracy for Vietnam. Broadcasting from an unidentified location in South Vietnam, the station featured a seductive female Annamese voice urging listeners to lay down their arms and go home. The script was vintage "Tokyo Rose" or "Axis Sally," classic World War Two propaganda radio operations, which sought to make Allied fighters homesick, long for loved ones, sick of war, distrust their leaders, hate their allies, distrust their weapons, fear the enemy's weapons. "Morale operations," in 1940s terms.

A little theatre will illustrate the way "Mother Vietnam" operated:

The scene is a rough camp in the jungles of South Vietnam. A dozen or so men and women dressed in black uniforms sit or lie around a small fire. AK-47s lean against a downed tree trunk. One of the group fiddles with a small transistor radio trying to tune in a scratchy signal. The signal turns into music, the music softens and a voice-over is heard:

"Good evening, fighters for the homeland. This is Mother Vietnam bringing you news and entertainment to help you in your patriotic struggle."

Bridge music up, then down:

"First news. In Hanoi today, patriotic citizens happily accepted reduced rice rations as the price for building the socialist state. Elsewhere our troops…"

At the end of the news, bridge music takes on a dirge-like quality then softens, and Mother Vietnam in voice-over:

"Mother has the sad duty to speak to the men and women of the 615 Sapper Company. Mother weeps for her sons and daughters who paid the ultimate price for the homeland at yesterday's heroic action at Anh Khe Pass. Mother grieves for Sergeant Ky Thai Ton, Sapper First Class Le Xuyen, Captain...."

After more music, "Letters from Home"--heavy on nostalgia. Following letters, a selection of folk songs or popular music familiar to all the country boys in uniform.

"Mother is here every night of the week, don't forget to tune in....Good night."

Then, if the propagandist has done his job well, in Act Two, one of the black-clad troopers (his morale in shambles) slips out of camp during the night, throws his rifle in a river and goes home, or gives up to the nearest ARVN unit.

The effectiveness of such operations has always been hard to measure. To get an idea of effectiveness, captured or surrendered soldiers are routinely asked if they listened to radio and if they were influenced to act by what they heard. The propagandist hopes the defectors will come in and say, "Oh, yes, your broadcast made me do it." The results of such audience polling often is inconclusive. We did not know if "Mother Vietnam" was effective when I arrived in Saigon.

ARRIVAL IN SAIGON

The Pan American 707 landed at Saigon's Tan Son Nhut airport just at dusk on September 7, 1973. It was dark by the time I cleared immigrations and customs and went to find transport into the city. Expecting to be met, I searched the crowd at the terminal entrance for a familiar face, found none and was about to take a taxi when I felt a hand on my shoulder. I turned to face an agency officer I had known slightly in years past, Carl Spooner, was returning from "FVT," governmentese for Family Visitation Travel (government paid visits home when officers are forced to live apart from families). Carl invited me to ride with him in the company car that came to meet him. We climbed into the Ford Falcon and headed for the city in a light rain.

Fifteen minutes later we were at the Duc Hotel, a six-story CIA hostel in mid-town Saigon that provided temporary lodging and mess facilities for newly arrived employees, staffers in from the provinces, and the large number of temporary-duty people who visited Saigon. The barbed wire and sandbagged bunkers at the hotel entrance signaled a city under siege. A porter took my bags from the trunk of the car and guided me to the front desk where I registered and was shown to a large room on the second floor. I washed up and was about ready to find the dining room when the telephone rang. It was Sam Banks, chief of the radio project. He invited me to come up to the rooftop bar for a drink.

Sam and I had worked together some years ago at headquarters, he had not changed much and I easily recognized him. He introduced me to Robert Sand, radio engineer to our project, and we sat down to an hour of getting acquainted and trading gossip and rumors. We continued our reunion in the hotel dining room. The Duc Hotel was one of the best places to eat in Saigon, thanks to the skills of the manager and premier chef, Oscar Milar, an old friend, who had managed CIA clubs at various Far East posts during the Cold War years.

After dinner Sam and Bob left me to surrender to my jet lag. The next day would be a heavy schedule of processing into the station and briefings on the radio operation.

Sam picked me up at eight o'clock the next morning and we drove through the bicycle-clogged streets to the U.S. Embassy, a fortress-like structure near the center of Saigon. Sam had arranged to begin my processing with an introduction to station chief Thomas Polgar.

A short, stocky man, Polgar spoke with the accent of his birth place, Hungary. He had come to the States in the thirties, escaping the Nazi pogroms. He served in the Office of Strategic Services (OSS) during World War Two. He joined CIA after the war and served with distinction throughout the cold war and was now chief of CIA's largest station.

The interview was brief, Polgar was courteous but not long on personal relations. He got right down to business and made clear that the radio operation was very important and he urged Sam and me to do our best to make it as effective as possible.

Sam and I left Polgar's office and drove about a quarter of a mile from the Embassy to a large warehouse in a walled compound at Number 7 Hung Tap Tu Street. The radio project was known as "House Seven" among US and Vietnamese officials; to the public, the compound was just another military installation with ARVN guards at the gate. The Psywar Command provided the real estate and Vietnamese staff; CIA provided funds for equipment, supplemental Vietnamese-staff salaries, psywar guidance and technical assistance. The House Seven staff numbered about two hundred Vietnamese: writers, researchers, translators, announcers, singers, musicians, actors, technicians, managers, housekeepers.

The senior Psywar Command officer at House Seven was Major Le Ngu, about forty, slim, rather taller than most Vietnamese. Stickler for rules and regulations, a worrier, but reasonable in the end.

Four CIA officers were assigned to the project. Chief was Sam Banks, about fifty, slim, medium height, thinning hair, good humored, long experience at propaganda radio operations and convinced of their effectiveness.

I was to be deputy. I brought to the project twenty-five years of intelligence and covert action experience, mostly targeted at Communist China. My main responsibility would be to provide thematic guidance to the writers and producers.

Our broadcast radio engineer was Robert Sand, fifty-five, a little heavier than he should be for his medium height, balding, longtime buddy to Sam, expert at his business. Bob was charged with keeping the radios on the air.

Peter Hart was our linguist--the rest of us only had a smattering of Vietnamese. Peter was twenty-five, married to a Vietnamese woman. He was tall, dark haired, good looking, serious and enthusiastic about his work. Peter monitored all of the broadcasts so that we could make sure they said what we wanted said. Peter also served as a check on the Psywar Command interpreter, Sergeant Tinh, Major Le's staff interpreter.

Sergeant Tinh Tran Dinh was about Peter's age, slim, medium height, of serious mien, rather diffident, spoke excellent English.

Mai Lan was "Mother Vietnam" and very much a key player, not only as the principal on-air voice, but also in designing the whole broadcast program. Mai was a beautiful young woman, about thirty, slim, athletic figure, enthusiastic, outgoing. She had worked earlier for Armed Forces Radio Saigon during the times of large US forces levels in Vietnam. She was a trained and skilled broadcaster.

One key player remains, Joseph Hamm, Canadian born contractor who built and maintained our studio and transmitters. Joe was a prototype of the tough, no-nonsense, hard drinking, do anything-to-get-the-job-done building contractor of which there were many in Vietnam serving the needs of the US agencies. Joe was about fifty, sandy haired, of medium height, accented by a beer belly. Joe had a remarkable vocabulary of four letter words.

This then was the project and the people I was sent to Vietnam to work with. Would it be an activity that would make a difference in the long struggle for peace in Vietnam? I had doubts from the beginning. I was not an expert on Vietnam, but I had followed the course of events there through the years. Indeed, Vietnam was such a dominant presence through the sixties and seventies that all CIA intelligence officers had to keep generally apprised of events there. My reading of the situation at the time I arrived in Saigon was that Hanoi was on a winning course and that Saigon and its allies could do nothing that would significantly change that course. I accepted the assignment as a good soldier--my reservations set aside. Further, with two children in college, the extra pay was welcome.

Entering on duty in Saigon was like going to a class reunion. I renewed contact with a number of old friends at the station, friends from Far East posts and several from my European assignments. Saigon Station gathered together a cross-section of CIA's people from all areas of world, most of them draftees filling their area division's quota to keep the Agency's largest station fully staffed. Most were on eighteen-month assignments without families and eager to get Vietnam behind them and to return to their families and to get on with their careers in their areas of expertise.

My wife, Lois, joined me in January 1974. She had remained in Chevy Chase to spend Christmas with our two children before coming to Saigon (Sara was at Carleton College in Minnesota and Andrew at Northfield Mount Hermon prep-school in Massachusetts).

Lois and I were quite comfortable at the Duc and regretted leaving when, after two months, we were assigned a house. The house on Phan Dinh Phoung street was a French colonial town house with large rooms, high ceilings, tile floors, air conditioning, surrounded by high walls and came with a staff of guards provided by the station. We inherited a cook from a departing family and were all set for a two-year tour of duty.

Soon after her arrival Lois was selected to head the foreign community's social welfare program. She supervised the distribution of a sizable amount of money contributed by the foreign community to be used to aid Vietnamese orphanages and other social service institutions in Saigon and other parts of South Vietnam. She traveled often on Air America C-47s and Huey helicopters to cities throughout the country to assess the needs of social service institutions and to control the use of funds, medicines, and other forms of aid she provided in the name of the International Women's Association. She was excellent at her work and gained a reputation for exacting quality care for the children she sought to help.

Among her many talents, Lois was also a physical therapist with considerable experience in the third world. She was drawn naturally back to the practice by the needs she encountered among the orphans and from this came a call for her to advise on physical therapy in several Saigon hospitals. She went on to establish a physical therapy department at Grall Hospital, training nurses to assume physical therapy tasks.

Beginning early in 1974, Saigon was considered safe enough so that families might join the men and women stationed in the city. The American Community School was reopened and grew in population and the need for teachers. Again, Lois was enlisted, this time to teach algebra and geometry.

Our children, Sara and Andrew came to spend the summer with us in Saigon. With only two bedrooms in our house, we arranged for Sara, the eldest, to stay at the Duc Hotel while Andrew occupied our second bedroom. Being early arrivals, both children were rewarded with jobs with the US mission. The embassy had created a small number of part-time jobs for the purpose of keeping young people occupied and out of trouble. Sara worked in the indigenous personnel office and Andrew worked for the Mission Warden, the security office. The two of them spent a good deal of their free time in the Buddhist community where they had an introduction to a Buddhist nun from a former teacher. At the end of summer they returned to school in the States.

Saigon was not to be a family post for long. The year 1974 saw the cease fire severely tested as Hanoi pursued its "war in peace" campaign of continuous attacks whereever they found Saigon forces vulnerable. Beginning with small scale actions to grab land and population in remote areas, the North Vietnamese Army (NVA) turned gradually to regimental size actions to position their forces for a major effort in 1975. In April 1974 the NVA sent two regiments against an ARVN outpost which blocked an infiltration route south of the Highlands city Pleiku. The South Vietnam forces beat off the attack and held its position. Two NVA divisions attempting to isolate Da Nang in July were repulsed. By December the military situation was reaching the boiling point. In the last week of December the NVA launched a two-division probe at Phuoc Long, a provincial capital seventy-five miles northeast of Saigon. ARVN forces held out for a week under heavy attack but by January 7 the North Vietnamese forces were in control of the city. This was the beginning of the end, although we did not realize it at the time.

Toward the end of January 1975 three NVA divisions were reported moving south toward Ban Me Thuot, a strategic town in the highlands. Here would come the turning point in the war.

Personal life goes on in the midst of war. In March, I became eligible for FVT to visit my children. The perk covered only me, Lois was not included in the government paid travel. She and I discussed the increasingly threatening military situation, I was reluctant to leave her to face the NVA without me, but we concluded the end was still some time off. We agreed also that the children needed parental contact. Lois had her work to which she was devoted and she had good friends nearby; she elected to stay in Saigon while I went off to visit the children.

I departed March 16th bound for Washington for the compulsory check-in at Headquarters, which I easily limited to one day as no one seemed much interested in hearing about radio operations in Vietnam.

Next stop Northfield, Minnesota, where Sara was in her third year at Carleton College, one of the country's best small liberal arts colleges. She had arranged lodging for me in the home of a retired professor. Sara and I had a good visit in that snowy prairie town, I met some of her professors and many of her friends, including one special young man. A serious student and a lover of nature, Sara was struggling with where to concentrate in all the learning open to her: literature, Japanese, psychology, environmental studies, French? Psychology was leading just then--encouraged by a dynamic young professor.

We read the war news together. Ban Me Thuot, a strategic town in the Central Highlands, had fallen, opening the way for communist forces to drive to the sea and cut South Vietnam in half. Sara and I agreed that I should return to Vietnam sooner.

I flew to San Francisco, hired a car and drove to Santa Cruz to visit Andrew at the University of California branch in that beautiful seaside town. I found my bearded son at his dormitory where I was greeted with bear-sized abrazos. In his first year, Andrew was an dedicated student of biology and environmental studies. I had arrived at a short break in classes and he had designed a tour of the coast south of Santa Cruz down to Big Sur, Carmel and Monterey. We had good talks as we drove along and I found him happy and making good progress on his studies. We had happy days. but the war news was a dark cloud over us and Andrew urged me to return to Vietnam earlier than we had originally planned.

I flew from San Francisco hoping that Tan Son Nhut would not be closed before I got there. I landed on April lst greeted by a calm Lois, completely unworried by war developments. She had been very busy working on "Operation Babylift," the large scale air evacuation of Vietnamese babies, orphans and adopted children to the States and elsewhere.

On April 4, Lois helped load 250 Vietnamese babies onto a US Air Force C-5A Galaxy, a huge cargo plane, destined for California. A number of DAO employees served as escorts for the babies. Lois was invited to go as escort also, but, because she did not have her passport with her, was left behind. The C-5A took off and just minutes into the flight lost a rear door which damaged control cables. The pilots turned back to Tan Son Nhut, could not make it, crash landed and broke up in a rice paddy five miles short of the runway. One hundred and thirty five babies and escorts died. Lois worked into the night helping to take care of the survivors as they were brought into the US military hospital. In the overwhelming sadness of the situation her spirits were buoyed when she found alive and uninjured a two-year-old girl she had helped friends in the States adopt.

EVACUATION PLANS

When I walk into Sam's office the day after my return from FVT, Bob and Peter were there and the three were talking about the rapidly deteriorating military situation. They were especially concerned about what would happen to the House Seven people if the communist took over. I offered the cheery estimate that any Vietnamese associated with CIA could expect the worst. It was obvious to all of us that we should prepare plans for rescuing our Vietnamese associates if and when the end came. We could not cut and run. House Seven would, of course, continue to do its duty -- continue on the air -- as long as the Saigon government held out. But at the same point we would have to get our people out.

We knew that plans for the evacuation of the Americans were well advanced, indeed, many Americans and many Vietnamese had already departed and more were leaving every day. All US agencies and US companies were cutting activities and sending personnel back to the States. US military authorities were putting finishing touches on "Operation Frequent Wind," a contingency plan for evacuating all official Americans from Vietnam. We knew also that the Saigon Station plans would permit a small number of what were labeled "Key Indigenous Personnel" (KIPs) to be allotted places in the evacuation scheme. For House Seven we might expect only about ten slots, meaning we would have to play God in naming names for those slots. Sam urged that we would have to do better than that. Clearly, we had a moral obligation to do all we could to safeguard our House Seven associates.

We had had a preview of what might happen in Saigon in the horror stories told by our colleagues about the evacuation of Da Nang just a few days earlier. Photos of Vietnamese, civilian and military, mobbing aircraft as they departed the large northern city were in our minds. We could see Saigon dissolving into chaos as the North Vietnamese forces approached the gates of the city. Saigon would not be the place to be at that time.

At that point in our discussion, I suggested a course of action that might work. I pointed out that we had a transmitter installation at Vung Tao, the small resort town on the South China Sea. Would it be possible to move the House Seven staff to Vung Tao, away from the potential for chaos of a city of two million, and carry on our broadcast activity there? On the edge of the sea, Vung Tao would offer the possibility of evacuation over the beach to boats and ships in the end. Sam and the others liked the idea. It offered hope and, while it would not be easy to move 150 employees and their families, we had to give it our best shot. We began planning the logistics of such a move: transport was available, there was space at the transmitter site for setting up a studio, the Psywar Command could find living quarters for our staff. Enthusiasm for the scheme grew as we worked over the details and were able to offer solutions for all difficulties we could envision.

Before going any further we would have to obtain command approval for the scheme, from both the American and Vietnamese chains of command. Sam took our hurried notes and went to Saigon Base chief Bill Mason -- our immediate boss -- the first rung in the chain of command. He liked the idea, as we were sure he would. The radio project was a high profile activity and a favorite of his among the activities under his command --Mason would do anything to preserve House Seven.

The next step was to clear the scheme with the Psywar Command's Colonel Dong Tran Van. The colonel agreed in principle that it was important to keep House Seven in the war and that the project should be moved to a safe location. But he pointed out a major obstacle: Vung Tao had become a refugee evacuation center and was over-crowded with restive refugees. Colonel Dong promised to explore other sites for relocation of House Seven.

In the meantime, at House Seven we continued our exploration of options for preserving the radios and our people. Bob suggested we find a ship. House Seven could broadcast from the sea, out of reach of the NVA. The idea fell of it own weight --there would not be time to locate a ship and make all the alterations that would be necessary. Move the project to The Philippines or to Thailand? No, those governments would not permit us to extend the war to their territory.

Two days later, Colonel Dong came to House Seven to propose a new home for House Seven. He placed a map on Sam's desk and pointed to an island in the Gulf of Siam off the west coast of the Delta: Phu Quoc Island. He told us that the island was also used for refugees, but was not crowded, and offered an abandoned former US military camp that could accommodate House Seven. The camp was near a Vietnamese naval base and an airstrip that would take Air America's C-47s. This site seemed perfect for our purposes. With the colonel's approval, Sam and Bob flew to the island in the afternoon to survey the base. They returned in the evening and pronounced Phu Quoc entirely satisfactory.

The plan was now ready for the next rung of approvals. Bill Mason took the proposal to Tom Polgar. The chief of station was very much concerned to keep the radio project viable as long as possible and to rescue its Vietnamese staff if it came to that. Polgar discussed the planned move with Ambassador Graham Martin. The ambassador at this stage was convinced that a negotiated end to the conflict could be arranged with Hanoi. He would brook no actions that would suggest a lessening of our support for the Saigon government. We must not appear to be running away from the fight. Polgar emphasized that far from running away, the move would keep the pyswar effort more surely in the war. The ambassador's concerns assuaged, Polgar approved the plan and preparations for the move got under way.

At this point Saigon Station was being down-sized and reorganized to meet the impending crisis. The advance of the NVA made it imperative to reduce staff whereever possible. The station began cutting all functions that were not essential and sending redundant personnel home. Personnel from the bases and outstations throughout Vietnam who had now become refugees because of the advance of the NVA were sent home.

On April 8 a defecting South Vietnamese pilot, flying an F-5, bombed the Presidential Palace in Saigon—a quarter of a mile from my house. This signaled to me it was time for Lois to follow the other dependents and get out of Vietnam. She was reluctant but good sense and the chief of station prevailed. She ran into Polgar on the street after the bombing. "Vat are you doing still here?" he asked. She boarded the last Air Vietnam flight out of Vietnam two days later. She would remain in the safe haven for dependents in Taiwan until my fate was settled.

In the shuffle of functions and people I was pulled out of House Seven and assigned to a special project under the supervision of the former chief of CIA's Nha Trang Base,Neil Rogers, an old friend from days when we both worked on China operations. Neil had lost his base to the advancing NVA just day earlier and was brought to the station to handle special projects. I was tasked with a project requiring the talents of a train propagandist. My job was to cull out information from the station's intelligence reporting that would present the military situation in the most optimistic light. By highlighting ARVN successes—if we could find any, we would hope to insure continued strong support to the Saigon regime.

Washington, the Congress and the American people, rapidly losing faith in its ally, had to be convinced that the Saigon regime still had a chance of holding on long enough to give the diplomats time to arrange a negotiated conclusion to the conflict and an honorable exit for the United States.

ARVN just at that moment was engaged in a spirited and briefly successful defense at Xuan Loc, a strategic road-crossing blocking the eastern approaches to Saigon. This one action was the only bright spot I could find in a dismal mosaic of defeats up and down the country. The hope generated a Xuan Loc was short lived, the town was taken by the NVA on April 15 following a massive artillery bombardment. The decimated ARVN units fell back toward Bien Hao, ten miles north of Saigon.

The relentless advance of the NVA made clear that it was time to put into effect the House Seven preservation scheme. On April 18 I was assigned back to the radio project. The deputy chief of station, Charles Pointer, called me into his office and told me all was in readiness for moving House Seven to Phu Quoc Island and he wanted me to go to the island soonest to establish the fall-back base. The movement of people would begin as soon as I signaled that Phu Quoc base was open for business.

I went to House Seven for a briefing from Sam on preparations for the move. Sam, Bob and Pete had got the radio staff ready for the move. Each of the 150 staffers would be allowed to bring immediate family members with them to the island. They would be permitted one bag of personal items per person. Arrangements were made for transporting staffers to Tan Son Nhut when the time was set. Air America scheduled its fleet of transport aircraft, the work-horse C-46s and C-47s,for the airlift to the island fall-back base. Broadcast equipment was packaged and ready for shipment. There seemed to be nothing more to do but get on with the plan. I would leave for Phu Quoc on Sunday, April 20, to establish the base.

I spent the next day, Saturday, April 19, sorting out the few possessions I had retained in Saigon after Lois departed for Taipei. I would end up leaving most of my clothing in the apartment across the street from the embassy compound that I had moved into after Lois left. I had to pack everything in one medium sized canvas suitcase and one shoulder bag. One of the most important items I placed in the bag was the medical kit my wife had made up for me before she departed Saigon; it contained everything from bandaids to traquilizers.

That evening I had drinks with colleagues in the lobby of the apartment building. Most of them had been declared non-essential and were preparing to leave Saigon for the United States on evacuation flights over the next few days. Dick Archer, a para-military officer, asked me if I had a weapon to take with me to Phu Quoc. I displayed the "cannon" the supply officer had issued me that afternoon -- a venerable old, heavy-as-lead, GI-issue Colt 45 automatic. A weapon reputed to be so inaccurate that it would be more effective thrown at the enemy than firing at him. Dick, offering his best professional advice, said, "You don't want to take that thing with you. You just give that to me, I'll return it to supply for you." He then produced from his baggage a Police Special 38, a small snub-nosed revolver that held five rounds and weighed almost nothing. He said, "Take this, it wont do much damage but its easier to lug around." I thanked Dick for his kindness. I placed the pistol in my shoulder bag and would have it with me almost constantly for the next two weeks.

I was never sure what use I might have for the little 38. I did not expect to fight off Vietcong guerrillas. I told myself the gun might be useful in the event of an individual threat from a dissaffected South Vietnamese or a robbery attempt. The 38 rested at peace in my bag for the remainder of the war.

In one last look around the apartment I spotted my tennis racket. What to do with my faithful old Wilson? Was I not going to a Navy base? Do Navy men play tennis? I strapped the racket to my bag. Now I was ready to travel.

PHU QUOC ISLAND

My alarm clock awakened me at six on the morning of April 20th. It was Sunday. I had to be at the airport for a nine o'clock takeoff. I showered, shaved and dressed, then walked across the street to the American embassy compound. The dining room in the embassy club was almost empty. I ate pancakes and bacon alone with only the Stars & Stripes for company.

The war news was bleak. Our side continued losing ground as communist forces tightened the ring around Saigon. The heroic ARVN defense of Xuan Loc, 35 miles northeast of Saigon, was about to crumble under the relentless pounding of the guns of three NVA divisions. ARVN infantry, with some reinforcements dispatched from Saigon, was still holding on the morning of April 20 but could not last much longer. The army was running out of effective forces. The fall of Xuan Loc would clear the way to Bien Hoa, then the Hanoi forces would be in position to mount an assault on Saigon. Forces available for the defense of the city amounted to less than three divisions, composed of remnants of decimated units, made up of exhausted troops. Saigon could not be defended much longer. In the face of this situation it was clear our psywar operation would have to leave Saigon as soon as possible if we were to continue in business.

Breakfast finished, I returned to the apartment to gather my bags and load them into my station-supplied Datsun. I drove alone through almost empty streets to Tan Son Nhut airport. Most of Saigon was sleeping, perhaps resting up for whatever might be coming in the next few days. No problem getting through the military checkpoint at the airport entrance—my documents still worked. I pulled into the Air America parking lot and parked beside the single story terminal building.

I took my bags out of the car and started my routine car securing procedure. I picked up the chain bolted to the floor, fed it through the steering wheel and attached the padlock through two links of the chain and snapped it shut. The snap stirred something in me. I thought: What am I doing? I won't be back this way again, I won't be using this car again. The war is over. The Saigon government will not be able to reverse its descent into history's dustbin. I would play out the charade of continuing the struggle from Phu Quoc Island, but what to do with this car? I looked at the key in my hand and considered what I should do with it. Securing the car at this stage of the game was ridiculous. I unlocked the chain, placed the key in the ignition and closed the door without locking it.

Comparing notes later with colleagues about what they did with their cars produced a variety of end games. Some locked their cars as usual and then threw the keys in sewers, into the river, into fields. Others took out or sabotaged the engine. Most would not make it easy for the communist to use these spoils of war. In the end Saigon Station left behind a fleet of Jeeps, Datsuns and Ford Falcons.

Joe Hamm and several of his workers were in the waiting room when I entered the terminal. Peter came in a few minutes later with Sgt Thinh. Thinh had gone with Sam and Bob when they made the first survey of Phu Quoc Island and would accompany me to introduce me to Captain Thieu, the Navy Base commander, and interpret if needed. He would then return to Saigon on the same plane and report to Sam any problems or unanticipated needs we might encounter on the island.

Peter told me he would be sending his wife's family with the House Seven group and asked me to look out for them. I promised to do so.

Joe announced that he would need to pick up some of his technicians who were at the Vung Tao transmitter site. This would mean a stop at the Vung Tao airstrip. I knew that Vung Tao was the objective of an NVA column that had occupied Phan Thiet, 50 miles up the coast, on April 18 and was pushing toward Vung Tao which the Saigon government had designated a refugee collection point. An estimated 50,000 refugees from Da Nang, Nha Trang and other northern areas were gathered in Vung Tao as we prepared to fly there on the

20th. ARVN was still in control of the town and most of the peninsula north of the town.

It was soon time to go. I said goodbye to Peter. Joe, Thinh and I, followed by Joe's crew, boarded the Air America C-47 which was configured for troops and cargo: bucket seats along the sides and plenty of space on the deck for cargo. We got off the ground at nine sharp, climbed to only about 5000 feet for the short bumpy flight. We were on the ground at Vung Tao in about twenty minutes. Vung Tao is the beach resort closest to Saigon and well known to a generation of American GIs as an R&R center and before them familiar to generations of French legionnaires who knew the town as Cap St. Jacques. A pleasant little village with tree lined streets beside a wide sandy beach. The restaurants and bars and other establishments that used to give pleasure to the soldiers and sailors were in depression on that April day. Vung Tao now is probably a favorite of off-duty North Vietnamese GIs.

We quickly loaded ten of Joe's people and their tools and personal gear. Before takeoff the pilot nonchalantly announced that we had one marginal engine. But, "Not to worry!" He thought it would be okay until he could get back to Saigon for repairs. I didn't say anything, but I wanted to get off and come on a later flight. But Vung Tao was no place to be at that time and there might not be another flight. I gritted my teeth as we raced down the airstrip. We were soon airborne and the pilot put the ship in a steep climb to get above SAM 7 range as quickly as possible.

It was a smooth flight across the unbroken green of the Delta, through cloudless skies. After a little over an hour we left the green behind and were over the Gulf of Siam and beginning to descend. Through the postage stamp window I could see the town of An Thoi which stretches along a wide bay at the southern tip of Phu Quoc Island. A single landing strip ran along the edge of the sea to the east of the town. We came around and made a smooth landing on the strip.

Phu Quoc Island is only five miles off the Cambodian coast just west of the Vietnam-Cambodia border. Shaped like a comma, the island is about 25 miles long, north to south, 15 miles wide at the northern side, narrowing to about two miles wide at the southern tip. The island is hilly and has large tracts of forest. The soil is fertile and produced rubber and pepper in colonial days. Fishing to supply the nuoc mam factories has been the mainstay of the economy in recent years. Vietnamese say Phu Quoc produces the best nuoc mam—the pungent fish sauce that gives character to Vietnamese food. Pnu Quoc Island has a place of distinction in the history of Vietnam: the Emperor Gia Long, founder of the imperial dynasty that ended with Bao Dai in our times, took refuge on the island during the Tay Son Uprising (1776-92).

Commander Tho, deputy chief of the Phu Quoc Military District, saluted and introduced himself when we climbed down from the C-47. He was short and a bit stocky, but very smart in his khaki uniform. He spoke excellent English. Later he told me of his training at US Navy training schools in the United States. The commander sized up our group then pointed to a 2 1/2 ton truck which he said would be for our use, along with the driver. We loaded the truck with Don's technicians and their gear and sent them off to the new House Seven compound. Then Commander Tho asked me to come with him to meet Captain Thieu, the commanding officer. Joe, Thinh and I climbed into Commander Tho's jeep and in three minutes we were at Military District Headquarters at An Thoi Naval Base.

The commander led us into the Headquarters building to a large office where he introduced us the commanding officer. Captain Thien was slim and taller than the average Vietnamese male, I figured him for a tennis player. He was smart and proper in his uniform and presented a confident mien. There could be no doubt: he was the commander. He too spoke excellent English, again a product of USN training in the United States and many years of contact with US military. He was courteous and welcomed us with cups of tea.

He began by telling us he had received a phone call that morning from Saigon authorizing our use of the abandoned military police camp. He said his resources were rather lean but he would provide all the help he could to support our (psychological warfare) mission. I thanked the captain and told him we would like to get right to work preparing the camp, the first contingent of House Seven people would be arriving the next day. I said the truck he had put at our command would be most helpful in transporting people and cargo from the airstrip to the camp. We might need additional trucks from time to time. He said he would try to meet that need. Now, Commander Tho could take us to the camp.

Joe, Thinh and I joined Tho in his jeep again and set out for the camp. We stopped at the airstrip so that Sgt. Thinh could return to Saigon on the plane that brought us and report that all was in order on Phu Quoc. The House Seven airlift could begin the next day, April 21.

As I was talking to Thinh in front of the air operations office, an English-speaking ARVN officer approached me. He introduced himself as Lieutenant Dong and said he was the air operations officer. He pointed to the AAM C-47 and asked my permission to send some people to Saigon on the plane, which would return empty except for Sgt. Thinh. I looked at the pilot and he looked at me. I instantly became the Air American operations director. We would do well to give all assistance possible to our Vietnamese benefactors. I told Lt. Dong to load as many passengers as the pilots could safely transport. The lieutenant signaled to a handful of Vietnamese soldiers to board the plane. Then he went into the air operations office and emerged a moment later with a group of twenty white-habited Vietnamese nuns and hurried them up the stairway onto the plane. The door closed and I waved to the pilot as he started taxiing out to the strip. He was in the air five minutes later.

CAMP SEVEN

Leaving the airstrip, Tho drove the jeep through the navy base, a complex of large sheds which housed the ship repair facilities, rows of quonset hut barracks and other one-story buildings. A sentry, an M-16 on his shoulder, saluted as we passed through the gate to the village of An Thoi which wrapped around the Navy base and stretched about half a mile along Cay Dira Bay in a grid three gravel-streets deep woven together by four or five cross streets. The streets were lined with small homes with red tile roofs. In the center of the town there were several taller brick buildings, with open fronts at the ground floor where merchants offered their goods: vegetables, meat, fish, fruit, clothing, pots and pans. One building housed a Chinese restaurant which we found produced passable meals and served the ubiquitous "Ba Mi Ba" beer, a staple since French days.

Leaving the village the gravel road climbed about one mile up to a ridge which walled off the town of An Thoi from the northern end of the island. Beyond the ridge, the road descended to a plain where it continued up the length of Phu Quoc to the northern end of the island, serving as the principal artery binding the island together.

About one mile beyond the ridge the road passed through a large military base which occupied both sides of the road with dozens of one-story barracks arrayed in ranks back from the road. This was the refugee camp which was rapidly filling with refugees from Da Nang, Nha Trang, Vung Tao, and Saigon.

We did not venture beyond the refugee camp during our stay on Phu Quoc. The military could not guarantee safety beyond that point. Vietcong guerillas were known to be present in the northern part of Phu Quoc. So far, Captain Thien's troops had been able to prevent any significant Vietcong infiltrations into the southern end of the island.

Our jeep labored and bumped along the gravel and much rutted surface to the top of the ridge where Commander Tho pulled to a stop at the entrance to a fenced compound which enclosed a large concrete block building. We dismounted from the jeep and passing through the gate, which was opened by a sentry, Tho, Joe and I entered the building. It was one large space about the size of a basketball court. Tho told us he had selected this installation to house our (psywar) broadcast studio. The location, on the highest point of the ridge was ideal for radio communications purposes. Joe and I agreed with his selection. The building would also serve as our communications center for contact with Saigon.

Commander Tho said he would have to leave us at this point and return to the base. We thanked him for his help and said we would take some time now to survey the situation and determine what remained to be done to prepare for the arrival of the House Seven staff which would begin the next day.

Joe instructed his technicians and workers to deposit their personal and technical gear in the building, which we began calling the Communications Center, or Comcenter. The workers were then set clearing some of the heavier debris from the barracks so the House Seven people could move in more easily.

Joe's communication technicians busied themselves setting up a single-side band transceiver and appropriate antennas to give us contact with Saigon.

The technicians also began preliminary planning for the installation of broadcast facilities and the construction of recording studios. We hoped to resume our psychological warfare operations as soon as a transmitter could be installed. House Seven in Saigon had prepared taped propaganda broadcasts in advance which could be aired without waiting for new studios. We planned to stay in the struggle as long as we could serve a useful purpose.

Joe and I headed for the former US military camp which would be the temporary home for the House Seven staff. We walked north on the main road just over the ridge where we turned onto a narrow gravel road which led off to the east, ending after about a quarter mile at a fenced compound. Much of the chainlink fence had fallen down and the gate was missing entirely. Inside the fenced area were ten one-story concrete-block barracks arranged in two rows extending to the east. Several smaller buildings which served as wash rooms were located at the end of the rows. There was a large open space the size of a football field below the barracks which probably had been a parade ground and sports field. The compound was surrounded by clumps of trees. From the east end of the camp a jeep trail led down hill about half a mile to a sandy beach on the Gulf of Thailand. During the height of the US military presence in Vietnam the camp had been occupied by a US Army military police battalion.

Joe's people were clearing most of the heavier debris out of the barracks. There would be more clearing for the House Seven to take care of. No glass remained in any of the windows and there were gaps in the roofs of several of the buildings. Joe and I calculated that the camp would accommodate at least a thousand people. If necessary, additional numbers could be housed in tents on the parade ground.

We never got around to assigning the camp a proper name. I call it Camp Seven throughout this account.

When we returned to the Comcenter, the cooks were preparing dinner for Joe's crew. The aroma of fried rice drifted through the concrete block building. Joe invited me to share their meal. The warm spicy food tasted exceptionally good after the long, busy and exciting day. Joe's team was very skilled in moving into a new situation, setting up camp and arranging for reasonably comfortable living while getting on with the project at hand. That was their job, they were builders, always on the move to a new project. Joe and his team and their skills were critical to the success of the House Seven evacuation.

After dinner I walked down the hill to the navy base. Commander Tho had arranged for me to spend the first night in the bachelor officer's quarters (BOQ). He guided me to what turned out to be a house trailer divided into four compartments, like ship's cabins. Each cabin had two beds with tick-covered mattresses, folded blankets emblazoned with

"US Navy," and little else besides some shelves for personal items. Tho indicated I should take one of the end compartments. The room was empty, I would have a private accommodation. Tho said goodnight, added that he would pick me up for breakfast and departed.

I stripped down to my underwear, placed my clothing on the shelf over the bed, made a pillow of my shoulder bag by placing soft items on top, and lay down and fell asleep immediately.

THE MOVE BEGINS

I awakened about six o'clock on the 21st to the sound of heavy rain. When I got my eyes open I noticed that the other bed in my compartment was now occupied by a softly snoring form. The insignia of rank on a shirt hanging on a peg above the form told me he was a Vietnamese navy lieutenant. I quietly put on my pants and shoes and, taking my shirt and shoulder bag, left the compartment and found the wash room where Tho had pointed the evening before. I took a cold shower, shaved and brushed my teeth. I finished dressing just as Tho appeared in the doorway to say, "Good morning."

The commander led me to the nearby officer's club. The dining room was very plain and unadorned except for a colorful Air Vietnam poster promising excitement in San Francisco. The room was rather dark, shaded to keep out the burning noontime sun. A number of plastic covered tables, each with an allotment of chairs, were scattered around the room. A few of the tables were occupied by groups of two or three men in navy uniforms.

Tho nodded to some of his colleagues as we entered the room, then selected a table. As soon as we sat down, an attractive Vietnamese woman of about forty years of age, dressed in an ao dai, the traditional long gown, approached our table and greeted Tho warmly in Vietnamese. He introduced her as the club manager, Ms. Bou, and invited her to join us. She addressed me in English: "Good morning. You like breakfast?" I said, "Yes, please." She then signaled a waiter to our table and ordered for us. Tho wanted only coffee, he had eaten earlier. The waiter returned quickly and placed mugs of hot coffee before Tho and me. Next came a plate containing two slices of bread between which was a thick slice of Spam; my breakfast. The coffee was black and bitter -- good navy coffee -- and the sandwich filling was not disagreeable.

Breakfast conversation among the three of us ran to get-acquainted talk: "Where you from in States?" "How long you been in Vietnam?" "You have children?" "You speak English very well." "Oh, you took training courses at San Diego Navy Base." "Yes, the military situation does not look good just now."

After a few minutes of pleasantries, I presented to Tho a problem Joe had brought to my attention the evening before. Joe had determined that the well at Camp Seven was not working, he would examine the pump this morning to see if it could be resuscitated, but until the water supply could be restored we would need to transport water to Camp Seven. I asked Tho if we might have a second truck to transport jerry tins of water from the water point at the refugee camp. The commander allowed that a second truck could be arranged. Tho called to a young officer seated at a nearby table, who came immediately to attention before the commander. Tho spoke briefly, the young man saluted and quickly left the dining room. We resumed our chat.

I ate quickly because I wanted to get to the Communication Center to learn if Joe had established radio contact with Saigon. I needed to know how soon the House Seven people would start arriving.

Tho and I bid Ms Bou good morning and exited the club. Near the front door we found the young officer standing beside a military truck, a driver sitting behind the wheel and the bed filled with 5-gallon jerry cans. Tho said, "Here is your truck. The driver will stay with you as long as you need him. He knows what to do." I thanked Tho, got in beside the driver and we proceeded up the hill to Camp Seven.

The rain had stopped and the day was clearing. Good flying weather, so there should be no delay in transporting House Seven to Phu Quoc.

I stopped the truck at the ComCenter to talk with Joe who told me there had been no messages from Saigon. We were not to know whether or not the transportation would begin this day.

But preparation had to go ahead. One of Joe's workers was assigned to work with the new driver to begin the flow of water to Camp Seven. Joe's man took my place beside the driver and they set out for the water point. They would spend the rest of the day shuttling between the water source, about a mile beyond the camp, where they would fill the jerry cans from a well then transport them to the camp where they would be emptied into large tanks or drums.

I stayed at the ComCenter waiting to learn from Saigon when the flights would begin. Our radio link with Saigon was working satisfactorily, at least, technically. We could raise Saigon when we needed to talk to the station and Saigon could call us when they had something to impart to us. Our call sign was Brandy 4, Saigon was Baker 1. We maintained a daily contact schedule (military time, 24-hour clock): 0830, 1400, 1630, and 2100 hours. I called Saigon twice during the morning but no one could tell me when the transportation would begin.

The first incoming flight announced itself. About eleven o'clock I heard the drone of an aircraft. I was still at the Comcenter and had no transportation to take me down to the airstrip. I discovered among Joe's equipment a small-wheeled bicycle which I immediately took hold of and started down the rutted, gravel road as fast as I dared. From my two-wheeler I saw the plane circling out over the bay and it passed directly over me as it made its final approach. I pushed the bike to top speed and reached the quonset hut terminal building just as the C-47 pulled onto the hardstand. I parked my bicycle beside the hut and walked to the still idling aircraft.

The engines stopped, the side door opened and Sgt. Thinh, a broad smile on his face, appeared in the opening. Behind him were other familiar House Seven faces and some unfamiliar small faces. Thinh had brought his wife and three children on the first flight. The stairway was rolled up to the door and the passengers began to deplane. I shook hands with Thinh, and behind him, Mr. Han, a young chap who played comic roles in our radio dramas, then Ms. Chan who worked in the research department. Other staffers came down the stairway with their families following, bemused expressions on their faces. Some had been sick during the flight; this was the first time most of them had ever flown. It was necessary now to get them to their new quarters a soon as possible, both to avoid attracting attention to them and to allow them to get settled and get over the trauma of the flight.

Sgt. Thinh told me the flight was pretty bumpy and he was happy to be on the ground. He said there were seventy people on this initial flight and the remainder of the House Seven staff had been organized into groups of similar size for subsequent flights.

Captain Thien and Commander Tho arrived at the this point to observe the beginning of the airlift. I walked over to greet them. I observed that there were seventy people on this sortie, many more than we could crowd onto one truck. I suggested that a second truck would help us get these people to the camp quicker and avoid attracting too much attention. Thien agreed and nodded to Tho who took the cue and spoke to Lt. Dong, the air operations officer. Dong went into the terminal hut to order up the truck. Satisfied that all was well, the two officers departed after urging me to call upon on them for any additional help we might need.

Joe arrived just at that point with the first of the navy trucks assigned to Camp Seven. He directed the driver to pull up beside the C-47 and I instructed the new arrivals to climb into the canvas covered bed of the vehicle. They secured their bags, placed them on the truck and climbed, with some difficulty into the high bed of the truck. I had to remind some of the House Seven men to help the less agile into the vehicle. We managed to get about half of the seventy men, women and children from this first flight, and their bags, onto the truck. The second truck appeared just as the first one was full and we loaded the remainder. I asked Joe to go with the trucks to the camp to get our people settled into their temporary home. I would remain at the airstrip to meet the unknown number of flights that would follow.

The pilot of the first aircraft, who reported to me after his plane was unloaded, had told me that several additional flights were scheduled out of Tan Son Nhut for Phu Quoc on the 21st, but he did not know how many or the precise schedule. The pilot asked if I had any passengers or cargo for the return flight. As happened when I arrived the day before, Lt. Dong was quick to request permission to send several people to Saigon. I put on my Air America hat and approved Dong's list. When they were loaded the C-47 took off.

Four Air America C-47s landed at An Thoi airstrip during the course of day, each delivering fifty to seventy House Seven staffers and their immediate families. The cargo holds of the aircraft also yielded cases of C-rations, bags of rice and crates of vegetables. One flight delivered a generator that would provide electric lights for Camp Seven, when the fuel to power the machine caught up with it.

A contingent of twelve Nung guards arrived on one of the afternoon sorties. The Nung people were a minority ethnic group from the mountains of Vietnam whose language was a dialect of Chinese. Nung men were considered good fighters and, because of their separateness from the Vietnamese, were widely used as guards by US agencies. We would employ this force, armed with M16 rifles, to control entry to Camp Seven and the Comcenter.

I remained at the airstrip most of the day, leaving only to have lunch with Joe's staff at the Commo Center. His gourmet cook again performed his miracles under field conditions. After eating, I walked over to Camp Seven to see how settling-in was going. The first two groups had moved into the bare buildings and were turning them into apartments, using sheets and blankets and cardboard to create family units. Some had started small wood fires and were preparing tea or cooking meals. Water was dispensed from rows of jerry cans that our navy friends were transporting into the camp. But the fresh water was only for drinking and cooking. For bathing and washing dishes the Camp Seven tenants had to take a short walk to the beach. Joe and some of the House Seven administrative staff had a going concern in operation on the hill above An Thoi.

I returned to the airstrip in time to meet the next incoming flight and to serve as Air America flight operations manager. However one of my pilots balked at my attempt to board some of Lt. Dong's passengers. He maintained he had no orders to board passengers at Phu Quoc. He was unable to see that these were extraordinary times, times to take reasonable initiatives. It made no difference to him that my mission depended on Vietnamese good will and assistance and his airplane could help keep that assistance coming. He returned empty to Saigon.

Just before the last C-47 flight for the day took off to return to Saigon, a slim, deeply tanned, young man in short-sleeved shirt and shorts, carrying a large shoulder bag, came up to me and introduced himself as John Matern. He said he was a medical doctor and was operating a small clinic at the refugee camp. He requested a ride to Saigon where he would report on the refugee situation to AID authorities and seek additional medical help and medicines for the burgeoning refugee population. He planned to return in a few days and resume his work on Phu Quoc. I told Matern that I was from the embassy and charged with evacuating our Vietnamese staff. I also said I was happy to know there was medical help on the island and hoped that we might call on him when he returned. He agreed readily. I saw him onto the waiting aircraft which soon was airborne. (Dr. Matern did not make it back to the island.)

As I left the airstrip to walk up to the Commo Center I found myself among a long stream of Vietnamese men, women and children all carrying suitcases and other forms of baggage. I turned back and went to Commander Tho's office to ask about the new arrivals. He asked me to step outside of the office with him and pointed to the beach along side the airstrip. Two LSTs were pulled up on the beach. They were the source of the line of people on the road; they were still pouring out of the wide gaping bow doors of the large ships. Tho told me the ships were Chinese Nationalist vessels assigned to evacuate refugees from the Vung Tao refugee collection center which had become hard pressed by advancing NVA forces. The refugees would be accommodated at the camp north of Camp Seven, he added. (The Taiwan government had aided South Vietnam in various ways during the years of the Indo-China wars. The LSTs were part of Taipei's final assistance to Saigon.)

Tho invited me to have dinner at the club with him and to spend another night in the BOQ. I accepted but said I would go up to Camp Seven first to check on the settling-in and to get any messages that might have come in from Saigon. I rejoined the refugee line snaking up the hill.

A11 was well in Camp Seven. Over three hundred souls had arrived this first day and were safe and making do at the camp. Most families were busy preparing an evening meal. Rice was cooking on many small wood fires, and Vietnamese were becoming familiar with the contents of C-ration cartons. The fruit cocktails were favorites of the children.

At the Commo Center, Joe advised that there had been no communications from Saigon. In Joe's words: "The (expletive deleted) haven't told us a (expletive deleted) thing." I, too, was not happy that Saigon was not supplying us more information on the transportation schedule and on the military situation. We were left in the dark as far as substantive information affecting the security of our operations. Our only source of information on military developments was the radio: we depended on VOA, BBC and Armed Forces Radio to alert us to events that might impact our mission.

I walked down the hill again to join Tho at the officer's club. The specialty of the evening was phu, noodle soup, liberally laced with nuoc mam. Again, Ms. Doo joined us at the table. She did not eat the phu, preferring a tumbler of scotch and water. The commander and I drank the Ba Mi Ba (translated "33").

I asked Tho about the mission of An Thoi naval base. He observed that the base had been fairly quiet in recent months. During the height of the war, An Thoi had the mission of interdicting the sea borne flow of men and supplies coming from Cambodia destined for the Vietcong. A fleet of small patrol craft operating out of the navy base patrolled the waters and rivers of the western coast of the Delta, carrying out search and destroy missions. US Navy and Coast Guard units were stationed at An Thoi to advise and assist the Vietnamese in this task until the Paris accords brought peace, a short lived peace, to the area. He told me that he and Captain Thien had both received training at Navy schools in the States as part of the military assistance program. Tho had obviously enjoyed his time in the US and took full advantage of the opportunity to travel and to polish his English.

It was ten o'clock when we broke up and went our separate ways. I retired to my trailer compartment unaware that one more Air America aircraft had landed at Phu Quoc--without the assistance of the "flight operations chief." I learned the next morning that Sam, Bob and Mai Lan had arrived just before dark, while I was having dinner with Tho. They came in on a twin-turbo prop Volpar executive aircraft which turned around immediately and returned to Saigon.

House Seven

The Duc (CIA) Hotel in Saigon

No. 494

DUC Association

ASSOCIATE

SIGNATURE Charles E. Taber

AUTHENTICATING SIGNATURE

Joseph M. Straub

The author's Duc Hotel membership card

The author's Alien Registration Card

VIỆT-NAM CÔNG-HÒA
BỘ GIAO-THÔNG
VÀ BƯU-ĐIỆN

BẰNG LÁI XE TỰ ĐỘNG
(NGOẠI GIAO)

SỐ 54678 B
Có hiệu lực tới ngày

TÊN, HỌ : CHARLES E.
TABER (MY)
ĐƯỢC THỪA-NHẬN LÁI XE : DU LỊCH

Saigon, ngày 29 tháng 10 năm 1973
CHÁNH SỰ VỤ
SỞ KẾ-HOẠCH và KHẢO-THÍ,

BÙI TRUNG HIẾU

AIR AMERICA, INC.

THE GRAY HOUSE
CLUB – HOSTEL
MEMBER SHIP
CARD

NUMBER	MEMBER'S NAME	DATE
949	Charles E. Taber	1974

The author's membership card for Air America,
the CIA-run airline in Asia.

A Saigon street scene

A Saigon scene

Vietnamese temple scenes

Photograph of author at official party.

CHINESE LST'S

April 22nd was sunny and cloudless. Up at about six o'clock, I bypassed breakfast at the officers club and tramped up the hill to have toast and coffee with Joe and his crew at the Commo Center. Joe told me that Sam and Bob had arrived last night and had moved into one of the small buildings in the camp. The two new arrivals joined us in the Commo Center a short time later. Over steaming cups of coffee, Sam and Bob described the situation in Saigon as verging on chaos as the evacuation got into full swing. Many Vietnamese were approaching their American friends and contacts trying to arrange to be included in the evacuation. The consulate was swamped with visa applicants, most of whom would be turned away. Tension was building in the city as the military situation continued to deteriorate, Sam observed, noting that Xuan Loc had fallen and there was very little to stop the NVA from reaching Saigon in the next few days. Ambassador Martin was clinging to the hope that Secretary of State Kissinger would succeed in bringing about a negotiated resolution of the situation that would permit an orderly evacuation of US personnel remaining in Vietnam.

The only thing Sam and Bob were upbeat about was the progress of the House Seven evacuation. Peter, with the aid of our Vietnamese partners, was handling the Saigon end: organizing House Seven staffers and their families into plane-load groups, transporting them to Tan Son Nhut by bus, loading the Air America planes and dispatching them to Phu Quoc. The process was working very well. Peter would come to the island with the final group, probably at the end of the week. Transmitters and studio equipment had been packaged and scheduled for delivery in the next few days so that we might hope to resume broadcasting as soon as possible. Time was running out for psychological warfare to have an affect, but we were committed to continue our role in the defense of South Vietnam.

Sam and Bob said they found all well at Camp Seven, the people were adjusting to living on concrete floors and preparing meals over small wood fires. The supply of water was adequate for the present.

Then Joe spoke up with a disappointing report: the pump at Camp Seven could not be repaired. His technicians had worked all night, pulling the pump from the well shaft, dismantling it, attempting to fabricate parts, but ending up unable to make it work. We would have to ask Saigon to try to find a pump to send to us.

It was about time for our 8:30 contact with Saigon so we got right onto the water problem. The call went something like this: "Baker One, Baker One, this is Brandy Four, Brandy Four. How do you hear me? Over."

Saigon came back: "Brandy Four, Brandy Four, this is Baker One, Baker One. I hear you five by five. How do you hear me? Over."

I told the Saigon operator we could hear him loud and clear. We could now dispense with radio-speak and I proceeded to tell him about our pump problem and requested a replacement pump be sent as soon as possible. I added that until the pump could be delivered we would be dependent on transporting water from the refugee camp. To make this process easier, I asked Saigon to send us a water buffalo--a large water tank on wheels that could be pulled behind a truck. This would be an improvement over the present process of filling dozens of jerry cans in the bed of the truck, then off-loading and distributing them at the camp. The water buffalo could be filled and pulled to the camp where our people could draw water directly from nozzles on the tank.

I requested also that Saigon send us a jeep; we needed transportation to run the many errands connected with managing a refugee operation. Saigon agreed to all our requests and promised deliverv as soon as possible.

Next item of business that morning was the Chinese LSTs that Tho had told me of the previous day. I suggested we call on the captains of the vessels. Since we still had no word from Saigon about our transportation in the event evacuation became necessary, we would do well to explore the possibility of hitching a ride on the LSTs.

Sam, Bob and I climbed onto the navy truck which was heading down to the airstrip to meet the incoming Air America C-47s and C-46s bringing more House Seven people. The first flight of the day was soon circling to land and the three of us greeted our Vietnamese colleagues and got them on their way to the camp. Then we headed for the beach where the LSTs were pulled up.

I asked the officer stationed at the ramp of LST 230 if we might speak to the captain. He assigned a seaman to escort us to the bridge where we met Captain Chen Yung-kun. I greeted him in Chinese. He welcomed us in Chinese then switched to excellent English, offering us coffee. Chairs were brought and we chatted on the bridge. I told Captain Chen. that we were representatives from the American Embassy in Saigon and that we were charged with the eventual evacuation of a large number of local employees of the embassy. I told him we would have transportation out by air or by ship when and if the time came to evacuate. But, as he knew as a military man, things sometimes don't go as planned. I asked if we might count on him to take us and our Vietnamese out of Vietnam if our transportation did not show up. Captain Chen replied that he would be at An Thoi two days more and would be at our disposal during that time. We thanked him and as we were departing he suggested we might like to visit his ship's store. We gratefully accepted and the captain asked a seaman to lead us below decks to the store.

The ship's store was pretty spare, a small broom closet with a few shelves stocked with candy bars, toothpaste and cigarettes--all American brands. I bought some candy bars and my colleagues bought several cartons of cigarettes.

We left the LST and walked back to the air strip where another aircraft had landed and was off-loading another fifty to seventy House Seven staffers and families. We hurried them onto the waiting trucks and off to the camp and I approved Lt. Dong's passenger list for the return flight to Saigon. We would have time to find some lunch before the next flight.

Joe revealed that his men had found a good Chinese restaurant in An Thoi and we all set off through the town. The villagers turned as we walked by and children came close to see the foreigners. The houses were mostly one--storied, wood framed structures with reed or tile roofs, some with vegetable gardens on the small lots. The green of the plants offered the only color in the otherwise dominant earth tones of the houses and dirt streets. We soon reached the center of town where there were several two story brick buildings with ground floor shops opening onto the street. The shops included a couple of general stores offering clothing, pots and pans, tools; several food shops; and a couple of bar/restaurants.

We found the recommended restaurant, identified by a "33" over the door. This was not the shop number but the logo for Ba Mi Ba beer. The entire width of the shop front was open to the street and a single large room extended into darkness at the rear. Several tables with chairs were placed around the room and there was a bar at one side with shelves behind it on which were several large bottle of Ba Mi Ba beer and some Chinese liquors. Vietnamese speaking customers occupied a couple of the tables.

We stepped into the room and took one of the empty tables. A short husky oriental man of middle years came from behind the bar and asked in Vietnamese what we would like. There was no menu. We started by ordering beer all around. When the proprietor returned with the beer, I tried to order noodles in Mandarin Chinese but got only a shaking head in response. It was then Joe's turn, he spoke enough Vietnamese to get us bowls of fried noodles with a little chopped pork and vegetables on top. Passable fare and inexpensive: two dollars for the beer, pennies for the noodles. We would eat here several times during our stay on Phu Ouoc.

After lunch, my three colleagues walked back up to the hill to keep in touch with our campers and to catch and solve problems as they must arise when hundreds of people try to establish a daily life in a strange situation.

I returned to the airstrip to resume my role as Air America director and welcoming committee for House Seven arrivals.

Three to five aircraft would land each of the next four days delivering twenty to seventy souls and tons of cargo. Hundreds of boxes of military rations, dozens of bags of rice, many crates of vegetables, boxes of medicines and a refrigerator for storing them. The jeep and two water buffalos and the water pump would arrive in the next two days via the C-47s and C-46s which seemed to have unlimited capacity to supply our needs.

Those venerable old two-engine cargo aircraft had flown the Hump on the China-Burma-India front and dropped paratroopers into Normandy helping mightily in winning World War II. The C-47, the military equivalent of the DC-3, began flying in the mid 1930s and the C-46, a look-alike product of the old Curtis-Wright company, took to the air in the early 1940s in response to the war. By the mid 1970, when these events take place, some of these planes were as much as 40 years old. They served on many fronts during the Cold War and were much used by Air America and earlier charter airlines employed in clandestine and special operations for CIA. They have an honorable pedigree.

After the departure of the last aircraft of April 22nd, I jumped on the running board of already loaded--overloaded might be a better word--truck and went up to the camp with the latest arrivals. The new people climbed down from the truck, blinked at what they saw, gathered their baggage and found places in the barracks for themselves.

The Nung guards had erected two large tents on the parade ground to serve as their quarters. Sam had suggested this separation of the Nungs in recognition of the attitude of some Vietnamese toward them. They had lived separately through the ages, we could not but go along under these circumstances.

I located Sam and Bob where they had taken up residence in a small building on the sea-side of the compound.

The building probably had been the camp headquarters when US troops occupied the camp. They invited me to move in with them, there were several rooms. I decided that it would be better for one of us to be near the radio. I would move into the Commo Center. I accepted their invitation to share their dinner: C-rations and some fruit from the market in An Thoi. There was scotch and water to wash it down.

Dinner finished, the three of us walked over to the Commo Center to make our last radio contact with Saigon for the day, the 2100 hours contact. The Saigon communicator advised us that there would be at least four flights the next day, weather permitting, and that a water buffalo was ready to go. I reported our contact with the Chinese LST and Captain Chen's offer to take us out if needed. I asked Saigon if firm arrangements had been made for our eventual evacuation. The answer was a disappointing, "No, but don't worry. We will arrange something in good time." We began to worry at that moment.

We signed off and Sam and Bob departed for Camp Seven. Joe's people had a surprise for me. They had scrounged up a camp bed and mosquito net and frame for me. I was delighted. I asked them to place the bed outside the building--the nights were mild and I preferred the fresh air to the stuffy building. In the event of rain, there was a covered hard stand that had protected a gasoline pump in earlier days. I would move under that cover on the one day it rained. A fine bedroom for my stay on Phu Quoc.

WATER AND THE JEEP

The first aircraft to land on Wednesday the 23rd was a C-47 with an extra wide door which, when the engines stopped, opened to reveal the front end of an olive colored jeep. Headquarters had acted promptly on our request for transportation. With considerable maneuvering and the help of a large forklift, the ground crew managed to lower the jeep to the ground. The jeep was followed by a buffalo, a 1000 gallon water tank mounted on a trailer. The two vehicles occupied much of the space in the plane, reducing the number of House Seven passengers to about twenty. When they had deplaned we loaded them onto the waiting truck, to which we had attached the buffalo, and sent them off to the camp.

By this time Bob, Sam and Joe had joined me at the airstrip, all eager to try out the jeep. We all jumped into the vehicle, Joe behind the wheel, and after a few false firings managed to get the motor humming. Joe headed up the hill to Camp Seven, entering the gate just behind the lumbering navy truck with the buffalo trailing behind.

After the people were unloaded, Sam suggested we put the buffalo into service immediately and instructed the driver to proceed to the water point at the refugee camp to fill the tank. This would become the daily routine: the driver would make several roundtrips each day, fill the buffalo at the water point, return to the camp, park the tank on the parade ground where our Vietnamese colleagues could draw water as they needed it.

The first time the tank was parked and available to supply water, the campers, containers in hand, mobbed the buffalo, making it difficult for anyone to get water. Vietnamese do not by nature queue up. Observing the melee, Sam suggested to some of the senior staffers that it would be more efficient if they were to form a line. Somewhat abashed, they got a queue organized.

The buffalo operation proved to be more critical than we expected. As Sam, Bob and I were observing the water process, Joe returned from having talked with his technicians who were working on the Camp Seven well. He had bad news. His men had determined that the well shaft was hopelessly blocked. The only way to restore water supply inside the camp would be to drill a new well. The good news was, an ARVN engineer company attached to Captain Thien's command had well drilling equipment and was, indeed, drilling additional wells at that moment for the refugee camps.

Our next move was obvious, we got into our jeep and drove north on the main road about one mile to a fenced compound in which was parked a number of bulldozers, road graders, air compressor trucks and other engineering equipment. A sign in Vietnamese and English confirmed that we had found the District Engineer for An Thoi.

The sentry at the gate saluted as we drove into the compound; no attempt to stop us. We drove about a hundred yards to a building we thought might be the headquarters. We walked through the open front door where a young officer came to attention. Joe asked in Vietnamese if we might see the commander. The officer stepped into an office at the back of the room and quickly returned followed by a short, bespectacled, thirties something, officer with a worried expression.

Captain Cong spoke English, introduced himself and invited us into his office where he seated us around a table. He ordered coffee. When all the cups were in place I introduced myself and my colleagues. The captain said he knew who we were and asked, "How can I help you?". Joe explained our well problem and asked if the engineer company might be able to help us. We then learned the reason behind District Engineer Cong's worried expression. He recited a list of large and small demands on his resources. The rapidly growing refugee population had outrun his capacity to provide engineering services. He was running the public works for a city of twenty thousand and growing. His well drilling equipment was fully booked for the indefinite future.

We decide to play our ace. On the way over to the district engineer, we had agreed that, as an inducement to cooperation, we might offer to take the commander and/or his family out of

Vietnam with us. Sam took the lead, it went something like this: "Captain Cong, you know as well as we do that the struggle for South Vietnam may be over soon. I don't know what your plans are, but, we are prepared to take you and your family out with us, when and if the time comes to evacuate."

Captain Cong thought for a moment, but only for a moment, and told us he could not think of abandoning his post but, yes, he would be interested in sending his family out of the country. He shook his head sadly and stated, "I cannot guarantee anything, but I will try to take care of your well as soon as I can." The deal struck, we said goodbye to Captain Cong. We would be in touch.

We drove back to the camp where I left my three colleagues and proceeded on to the airstrip to handle incoming flights. Three additional flights landed during the afternoon. In addition to people, the aircraft delivered to us a large generator, two drums of gasoline for the jeep, one additional buffalo, and food supplies. By the end of this third day of transportation, we had over one thousand House Seven staffers and family members in camp.

With the departure of the last flight for the day I returned to the Commo Center. My three colleagues were there listening to BBC. They had some startling news: Nguyen Van Thieu had resigned the presidency, honing that his departure, long demanded by Hanoi, might facilitate a negotiated end to the fighting. Vice President Tran Van Huang had assumed control of the Saigon government. To the four of us this looked like the beginning of the end. The question of our transportation out of Vietnam took on a new urgency.

Another report added to our concerns: panic in the refugee camps at Vung Tao had produced rioting which government troops only just barely contained. Our thoughts turned to the burgeoning refugee camps just to the north of us -- most of those people had been shipped down from Vung Tao. What could we expect from them at the time of evacuation?

USNS RINCON

Commander Tho came up to me at the airstrip on April 24 as I was handling the first House Seven flight for the day. He told me that a US Navy tanker had just pulled into An Thoi harbor and was anchored off shore. I asked if I might have a boat to go out to the ship and consult with the skipper. Tho nodded toward his jeep, we climbed in and he drove to the navy dock where he arranged for a launch to take me to the tanker.

Fifteen minutes later as we approached the vessel I could see the ship's name plate--USNS Rincon. She was a small tanker, not more than 150 feet in length. and she was low in the water. My Vietnamese navy crew brought the launch along side and I went up the ladder.

A middle aged officer greeted me at the too of the ladder and introduced himself, "I am Captain Gile, welcome aboard." I introduced myself and explained that I was from the US embassy in Saigon and that I and my colleagues were responsible for the evacuation of about 1300 Vietnamese local employees of the US mission in Vietnam. I told him also that, because our evacuation plans were still uncertain, I made it my business to contact all ships calling at An Thoi to explore the possibility of enlisting assistance when the time to pull out came.

Gile allowed that a tanker was not an ideal vessel for transporting people but that he would be glad to help if we needed him. He said he could probably deck-load about 700 people and could reach Satahip, Thailand in about 24 hours to set the people on shore. I thanked the captain and said we might well take him up on his offer.

Captain Gile told me his ship was a reserve tanker that had been called up for evacuation duty. He said he and his officers were US Naval Reserve personnel and the crew was a civil service crew. They were doing their reserved duty on assignment to the evacuation command and had sailed their ship from New Orleans where they all worked in civilian jobs.

The ship's tanks were fully loaded: 20,000 barrels of JP4 aircraft fuel, 5,000 barrels of gasoline, 5,000 barrels of diesel fuel. He said the fuel was to support air operations out of An Thoi airstrip. According to Gile, the evacuation command was planning to use the airstrip as a standby air evacuation point for people in the Delta. The fuel was consigned to Captain Thien but there was one sizable hitch: there were no tanks on shore to receive the fuel. Captain Thien might be able to store some of the fuel in a few tanker trucks available to him, but that would not help very much.

Captain Gile said there was a possibility for storing the fuel on shore. He explained that the military uses large rubber bladders for POL storage where proper tanks are not available. These come in 10,000 and 20,000 gallon capacities. He asked if I might arrange to have some of these flown in to take the fuel on shore. I said I would radio our headquarters in Saigon as soon as I got back on shore.

Before I returned to the island. Captain Gile and I exchanged radio frequencies and agreed on a contact schedule when each side would listen for messages from the other.

As I went down the ladder to my launch Captain Gile assured me he would not leave Phu Quoc until our transportation was assured. I rode back to the island much buoyed by this solid potential for escaping Vietnam.

Back on shore I went immediately to Camp Seven to brief my colleagues on what I learned on the Rincon. At the camp I saw Sam standing near the water buffalo engaged in a rather heated conversation with a number of our Vietnamese staffers. After a few minutes he left the group and motioned me to come to his building where he filled me in on the problem: conflict between the Vietnamese and the Nung guards. Unfortunately, some of our sophisticated Saigon people had an attitude common among Vietnamese that the Nungs were a lower order of the human species, country bumpkins, and an alien race besides, who did not speak their language. The House Seven people were having trouble sharing rations equally with the guards and allowing them free access to the water buffalos. Sam was making it clear that the Nungs were part of our company and would be treated fairly. He attempted to shame the Vietnamese, probably with little lasting affect.

My Rincon story was welcome news to Sam, and to Bob and Joe, who had joined us in Sam's quarters. Joe pointed out that the two Chinese LSTs had departed, leaving us with only the Rincon as a certain evacuation vehicle. One certainty where very little was certain about our eventual departure from Vietnam; Saigon Station still had not advised us of definite plans for our exit. It was time for another attempt to find out what our bosses had in mind for us. We went all together to the Commo Center for our scheduled radio contact with Saigon.

I reported the arrival of the Rincon and what I had learned from talking with Captain Gile. Our people in Saigon knew nothing of the Rincon, it was not in their plans. As to their plans for the Phu Quoc base, there were none. "Hang in," was all the communicator on the Saigon end could say. I requested the POL storage bladders and received the reply that they would try to find and deliver them to us. End of communication. Morale was not good at Phu Quoc base.

I returned to the airstrip, several flights were scheduled for the afternoon.

THE AMERICAN CHALLENGER

Commander Tho drove up to the camp late morning on the 28th to tell us that an American freighter had arrived at An Thoi Bay during the morning. With the help of Captain Thien's landing crafts which were landing 8000 refugees from Vung Tao. The ship was the American Challenger, an 8,000 ton U.S. lines freighter under contract to the U.S. military sea lift for Vietnam evacuation operations. I arranged with Commander Tho to take a launch out to the ship. A Captain Arthur Boucher met me at the top of the boarding ladder. He was a tall rugged featured man. I introduced myself as a representative of the American Embassy in Saigon. I showed him my diplomatic passport. He then asked me to follow him to the bridge where he invited me to join him in a cup of coffee which we each ladled from a large pot.

We stood as we talked. I asked him if he was sent to take us off from Phu Quoc. He said he had no such orders by that he would be glad to take us if Saigon air lift command agreed. I asked him how long he would remain in An Thoi. He did not know as he had not received his next assignment. He noted that he would be in contact with the command during the morning and would report our request. I told him that I would return to shore to contact the embassy to confirm whether or not we should plan on leaving on the American Challenger.

Thus, with some reluctance I took the launch back to Phu Quoc. The Captain suggested that we have a communication plan. I told him that I would let him know my findings from contact with the embassy. I then returned to the launch which took me back to Phu Quoc and Camp 7 to brief my colleagues.

It was also on the morning of April 28 that we had our first and only helicopter visit. A huge Chinook machine with two large rotors brought 17 Vietnamese staffers from Rock Gis, one of our bases in the delta. The banana shaped chopper stayed only long enough to unload its passengers and then took off to return to its base. Headquarters had decided to make greater use of Phu Quoc as a staging area for the U.S. final evacuation. Unfortunately this decision came just a bit too late as Tan So Nut Airport in Saigon was actually already out of commission.

CAPTAIN THIEN

Captain Thien approached me at the air terminal shortly after I had taken care of the first flight of the afternoon. He asked if there were any problems and I told him all was going well. He then asked me to bring my colleagues to dinner with his family that evening. I told him we would be delighted to come and observed that our food provisions had been rather lean. He smiled and said come about six thirty.

I informed the others of our good fortune. We would have to make ourselves presentable for this command performance. We had been dressing for the field, shorts and work shirts and boots. I had decided the first morning on the island to grow a beard and had a good start by the time of this invitation. That would have to be sacrificed now. After meeting the last flight for the 24th I drove the jeep to a fairly isolated section of the beach at the end of the airstrip. I stripped off and waded into the water with soap in hand. After my bath, with the help of the jeep's rearview mirror, I shaved the beard off. I changed into clean clothing from my musette bag.

I drove back to the camp to collect my colleagues and we presented ourselves at the captain's house at half past six. Captain Thien greeted us at the door and introduced his wife, a very attractive woman dressed in the traditional ao dai. She spoke English and proved to be a charming hostess. The Thiens also presented two of their children to us, a daughter in early twenties and a teenaged son. Both spoke some English but were rather shy and spoke little during the evening.

The captain offered scotch, Cutty Sark, or beer, Budweiser. I took beer, my colleages, all three, drank scotch along with the captain and Mrs Thien. We sat in a sunny room in rattan chairs around a low table which held dishes of salty chips and small meat dumplings and several small bowls of nuoc mam.

The long sitting room was all windows on one side looking out at the sea and the islands of Cai Dira Bay. The room's furnishings were modest but attractive. There were paintings on the walls, flowers and seascapes, as I remember. A quality high-fi system provided a mix of American and Vietnamese music during the evening. At the far end of the room was a table set for dinner in the Chinese style, with rice bowls and chop sticks.

Our conversation avoided the war for the most part. The talk was mostly personal. They wanted to know about us: where we came from in the states, were we married, did we have children, how we liked Vietnam. We learned about the Thiens in the exchange. Thien had attended training courses in the States, Mrs Thien had visited California. Both were originally from Hanoi. Thien had worked extensively with the US military, especially the navy and the coast guard. The US Navy and Coast Guard maintained a base at An Thoi during the high period of the war and had provided the coastal patrol vessels which Thien now commanded (I learned later that Senator John Kerry had served at An Thoi as a naval officer).

After an excellent dinner of Vietnamese specialties and good French wine we stayed at the table and talked for about twenty minutes about the war. Thien was realistic about the prospects for the Saigon forces; he knew the end was in sight. We agreed that our days on Phu Quoc were sharply numbered. Sam and I made it clear to Thien that we would be happy to take his family with us if he would like them out of Vietnam, when and if the end came for his government. He said, nodding his head gravely, that he had his duty to perform and could not think of leaving, but, yes, he would like to send his family out with us. He added that he would appreciate it if we would also take Commander Tho's family and the families of some of his other officers. We readily agreed. There was not much else to say. We expressed our gratitude to Captain and Mrs Thien and returned to Camp Seven.

GET OUT ANY WAY YOU CAN

I was up with the first light on the morning of the 29th. Sleeping in the open I always got the first light and was usually up before anyone else. I had a feeling that something was about to break and I had better be up and ready.

Mr. Khang, one of Joe's English-speaking technicians, came up to me while I was brushing my teeth at the wash stand in the Commo Center courtyard. He was obviously excited about something. I said, "Good morning. What's new?" He said, "There's big news," and went on to tell me that General Duong Van Minh, "Big Minh," had just made a "big speech" on Radio Saigon. According to Khang, President Minh had informed the people of South Vietnam that he had communicated to the Hanoi government that he was ready to negotiate an end to hostilities. Big Minh said also that he had notified the American ambassador that all Americans should be ordered to leave Vietnam within twenty-four hours.

I knew that the General Assembly in Saigon had named "Big" Minh president just the day before, after Hanoi had hinted they might be willing to negotiate with the retired general. So this was it, the news we had been expecting.

Khang looked at me for a response. Stunned, all I could say was thanks. Khang shrugged and went back into the Commo Center. As I finished brushing my teeth a flood of thoughts raced through my head. The short notice was a shock--twenty-four hours to get out of Vietnam. Of course, my colleagues and I had expected this day would come but we had thought we would have more time. Our planning had been good so far. We had succeeded in transporting most of our House Seven people to the relative safety of Phu Quoc Island ahead of the mounting crisis in Saigon. We were positioned for easy evacuation when the time came. Now the moment had come. I felt a chaos in my heart. How were we to transport ourselves and our 1300 people out of Vietnamese territory before the Vietcong/North Vietnamese descended upon us?

The fear and uncertainty in my mind was then joined by anger. What happened to Saigon Station? Why did we have to learn of the expulsion order from a Vietnamese radio newscast? Why didn't our command inform us about Big Minh's order and lay out a solid, secure and well-thought out plan for transporting us out of Vietnam. But then I remembered why we had come to Phu Quoc--we had expected that Saigon Station might be in some disarray when the crunch came. We were right. Now we had a serious job to do. The evacuation was upon us.

After a couple of minutes I went into the Commo Center to find Joe. I could see from his face that Khang had already given him the radio news. He pointed to a steaming cup of coffee and said, "Drink it, you look like you need it." I took a few sips but it was too hot. I put it down. I told Joe we had better get over to Captain Thien's office to work out what to do now. We got into the jeep, drove over to the camp to pick up Sam and Bob and headed down the hill to the navy base.

Thien stood behind his large wooden desk when we entered the office. He greeted us and asked us to sit around a conference table. An aide appeared with cups of coffee which he placed in front of us. Thien repeated the news from Saigon and told us he had received orders from his headquarters to give us every assistance in leaving Vietnamese territory. He assumed that we would leave with the House Seven people on the American Challenger. He had a plan ready. The evacuation would begin after dark that evening. All Phu Quoc was on a dusk to dawn curfew. All local inhabitants and the people at the refugee camp were required to remain in their homes or barracks throughout the curfew hours. After dark there should be little danger of interference in our movement off the island. We should be able to avoid the intrusion of masses of refugees attempting to board evacuation vehicles such as occurred during the evacuation of Da Nang.

Continuing with his plan, Thien said he would send navy trucks to the House Seven compound after dark to transport our people from the compound to the beach where landing craft would take them to the American Challenger, at anchor about five miles off shore. This would require many truck roundtrips to carry our 1300 people to the beach, and then several trips by the landing craft to complete the transfer of people to the ship. It would be an all-night operation and we would have to keep to a good pace to complete the job by dawn. Although curfew would keep all local Vietnamese in their houses throughout the night they would hear the trucks and probably guess what was going on but they should not offer a threat to the evacuation.

We all agreed that the plan was sound and that we should begin preparations immediately. Before we left the office to get to work, I stated that we should coordinate the plan with Captain Boucher of the American Challenger. I asked Captain Thien for a boat to go out to the ship. Thien nodded to Commander Tho who signaled me to follow him. A short jeep ride and we were at the navy pier. Tho guided me to a navy launch at the end of the pier, spoke to the two sailors in charge of the boat, and waved goodbye as we pulled away and headed for the American Challenger.

I made the leap from the bouncing launch to the landing platform with help of Challenger First Officer Kukeas who then led me up the ladder to the deck and then to the bridge. Captain Boucher was waiting for me. I told Captain Boucher about the order for all Americans to leave Vietnam. He had already received that information from the (Frequent Wind) Evacuation Control Center. I said that it looked like we would need to evacuate our people on his ship. I explained that we did not yet have approval from the embassy to use his ship but that we would have an okay before nightfall. He said he had no specific orders about our group but would be happy to take us. He would seek approval from the Evacuation Command immediately. I told the captain that the Vietnamese navy would transport our people to his ship via landing craft after dark and that there would be about 1300. We agreed to communicate during the day via radio to verify our plans. I then returned to shore.

When I arrived at the Commo Center, Joe's radio operator was having trouble raising Saigon station--"Baker One" did not respond to repeated calls. I told the operator to keep trying. Four hours later, about three o'clock in the afternoon, we finally got through. I recognized the voice of Tony Collins, one of the key evacuation planners, on "Baker One." I took the microphone and told Tony we were getting pretty nervous about the communications failure. Tony explained what had happened to our communications net: the embassy parking lot, he said, was to be one of the main helicopter landing zones for evacuating the embassy staff. Blocking the way was a large tree in the middle of the lot, a beautiful tamarind tree, that was much admired by everybody, but especially by Ambassador Martin. The evacuation planners had told the ambassador the tree would have to go, but Martin said it should only be cut as a last resort and at the last possible minute. The minute had come and the tree was cut down and in falling broke the antenna used in communicating with Phu Quoc. The antenna was now back in place.

I briefly explained the situation on Phu Quoc. I told Tony that the American Challenger was still at An Thoi and that the captain agreed to take our people on board. I asked if the ship had been sent specifically to evacuate our group. Tony said the ship had not been sent for us. I asked what arrangements had been made for getting us off of Phu Quoc. Tony said he did not know what the plans for us were. That being the case, I asked could we use the American Challenger. The response was: "Things have fallen apart a little sooner than we expected. Get out any way you can."

I will never forget those words: "Get out any way you can." Saigon Station had not completed plans for our transportation out of Vietnam. It was a shock; Saigon had let us down. There was no time for me to say what I thought of Saigon's management of the situation. I just said, "Okay, we will arrange to pull out on the American Challenger." I then told Collins that we had already asked Captain Boucher to seek

Evacuation Command approval to take us and he was doing so. I requested that Saigon also communicate with Evacuation Command to make sure there would be no slip up on getting approval for us to ship out on the American Challenger. Tony agreed and assured me that Saigon Station would take action immediately. I signed off knowing we were on our own.

I then asked the radio operator to connect us with the American Challenger. When we got through to Captain Boucher, I told him I had approval from Saigon to exit on his ship. He said fine but added that because of atmospheric conditions he was having trouble getting through to the command. He assured us he was not going anywhere and that he would get the okay to take us with him when he sailed out of An Thoi harbor.

The House Seven people had to be prepared for departure. Joe and I walked the quarter mile to the camp to discuss with Sam and Bob our next moves. We decided to wait until late afternoon before telling the House Seven staffers about the plan to move out. We decided it was important that our plans not spread outside the camp. We knew that with such a large group of people it was probably impossible to prevent loose talk about our departure plans. By waiting we could perhaps limit leakage of our plans.

About four in the afternoon we began to pass the word. We walked through the camp and talked with heads of the various departments of the broadcasting operation. We told them of the plan to leave that night and instructed them to spread the word among their staff members. We tried to impress upon them the importance of preventing word leaking out to the huge refugee camp up the road. We reminded them of the chaotic conditions that plagued the evacuation from Da Nang when masses of refugees mobbed the evacuation vessels and planes. We asked them to instruct their people to prepare one small bag to take with them on the trucks that would transport them to the harbor. Larger bags--they were allowed only one each--were to be collected in one place to be brought along after all the people were safely on board the ship.

As I walked through the camp I could feel the excitement as the 1300 men, women and children began their preparations. They were making hard choices about what to take with them. Many had cheated on the baggage limits we had placed on them when we Phu Quoc. The extras had now to be brought them t discarded. Things of monetary value would have priority for space in those small bags to be held close as they would board the trucks that evening. Many had gold rings and gold bars and small object d'art as well as US dollars. Before leaving Saigon they had converted property and possessions into transportable valuables. The children too had their priorities. I saw one little boy carefully stuffing a dirty panda bear into his mother's canvas shoulder bag.

Unfortunately, all this activity and the rising noise level that went with it could not have escaped the notice of An Thoi town people and the refugee masses in the camp to the north of us. These activities went on through the rest of the day. Simple evening meals were prepared family by family and tucked into what must have been nervous stomachs. The cooking fires were dowsed. Dusk came on and, unlike most nights during the last two weeks, very few candles or oil lamps or battery powered lights were brought out. A flashlight here and there moved briefly then turned off. The camp became strangely quiet; only low murmuring could be heard. Then the waiting began.

The trucks were due to arrive at Camp Seven as soon as it was thoroughly dark. We began our vigil as soon as the sun went down, a little after six. Seven came and it was quite dark, but no trucks. Eight o'clock and still no trucks. It could not have been darker, we were all quite certain about that. About half past eight we heard the grinding engines of what had to be several large trucks coming toward us. No lights, the big six-by-six trucks lurched slowly into the camp and stopped. Six canvas covered trucks. Sam, Bob and I assembled our people in truck load groups and asked them to climb into the beds of the vehicles. There was a rush to get on board the first trucks. To speed the travel to the beach we would fill the trucks to capacity in order to reduce the number of trips necessary to get all to the beach. Fortunately, Vietnamese are small people, especially the women and children. We were able to crowd about fifty people on each truck. The six trucks would take about three hundred.

Everyone wanted to be first to board the trucks. In spite of the chaos they sorted themselves out and filled up the trucks. With the first convoy loaded, I climbed into the cab of the first truck to lead the first increment to the ship.

The trucks rumbled slowly down the hill on the main road, then through the streets of An Thoi town. No one was on the street--the curfew had sent all townspeople to their homes at six o'clock. Oil lamps flickered through the windows of the small wood and stucco houses. Lamps outlined figures at some of the windows. The villagers were watching the show in the darkness. We drove past the navy base, past sentries posted at the gates. They eyed our convoy as we passed. My driver then turned down toward the beach on the west side of the air strip. The driver applied squeaky brakes and we came to a halt at the top edge of the beach.

Drawn up on the beach was a large landing craft with its bow door open and the landing ramp down. I looked into the deck and began to calculate how many of our people we could jam into that space. I estimated we could squeeze about 500 on board and would probably need three trips to get all House Seven people from the beach to the American Challenger. (Later; I identified the vessel in Jane's All the World's Fighting Ships as a Landing Ship Utility or LSU. It measured 119 feet in length and had a beam of 34 feet.)

Two spotlights on the bow of the landing ship illuminated the beach area in front of the landing ramp. Several Vietnamese sailors stood in the bow door. Clusters of ARVN soldiers stood off to the sides on the beach. No one appeared to be in charge. No one came forward as I walked down the beach toward the ship. I looked around for Captain Thien or Commander Tho but found neither. This was a bit strange but I felt we had to keep the operation moving. I instructed our people to climb down so that the trucks could return to the camp for another load. I had the House Seven staffers gather at the top of the beach about fifty yards from the LSU. The trucks pulled out as soon as they were unloaded and headed back up the hill leaving me and the nervous three hundred in the dark at the edge of the beach.

I decided to get the first group loaded onto the LSU and directed them to follow me down the beach to the door of the ship. As I started down the beach the ARVN troopers spread themselves in a line across the front of the LSU ramp, holding their M 16s at the ready. An officer appeared in front of the line of soldiers.

What was going on here?! I thought all arrangements had been made for our evacuation. I asked Sgt Thinh, House Seven's chief interpreter, to come with me and I walked up to the officer. I explained to the young lieutenant that Captain Thien had arranged for me and my people to be transported to the American Challenger on the LSU. The lieutenant said he knew nothing of any such plans. He said we could not board the vessel.

Fear flooded my heart at that moment. Was one of the nightmares I had been having since landing on Phu Quoc coming true? Were these disgruntled and resentful Vietnamese turning on their American allies for abandoning them when the chips were finally down. Or could it be an ARVN squeeze operation? Worse, could these troops be Vietcong in ARVN disguise? Or ARVN opportunists collecting bargaining chips--four Americans imperialists and a staff of Vietnamese collaborators--to offer the communists in exchange for favors when the new regime takes power.

The need for action took over and suppressed my fears. I asked the lieutenant to take me to his commanding officer. This worked. He led me and Sgt Thinh to a jeep at the top of the beach.

As we walked past the House Seven people I heard nervous whispers and could see fear in their eyes. They were having the same kind of thoughts I had just had. Where was Mr. T going? Would he come back? I had to do something to reassure them. I told them I was going to straighten out the difficulty and would be back soon. I told them all to sit down on the beach and be calm. All would be okay.

Sgt Thinh and I got into the jeep with the lieutenant. As we pulled onto the road I looked back and saw three hundred dark shapes squatting on the sand.

We drove for about two minutes and pulled into a military compound and stopped in front of a one-story wooden building. The lieutenant led Sgt Thinh and me into the building which consisted of one large room furnished only with a couple of tables used as desks.

Three kerosene lanterns produced a dim light in the room. We were brought in front of one of the table-desks behind which sat a major.

The lieutenant saluted, then spoke in rapid Vietnamese to the major. The major turned to me and asked in accented English, "How can I help you?" I told him what had happened at the beach and then told him that Captain Thien had authorized our departure from Phu Quoc, using the landing craft to transport our people to the American Challenger. The major was also in the dark about plans for the Americans and their Vietnamese charges. He would have to phone Captain Thien. The major cranked the field telephone at the side of his desk. No response. He cranked again. Again no response. He looked at me and shrugged his shoulders. "Much trouble with the line," he said. He cranked again. This time he got someone on the other end of the line and asked for the Captain. Again we waited for the connection to be made.

"Captain Thien is not in his office," said the major, glancing toward me after speaking briefly on the phone. It was not a particularly hot night but I could feel sweat coursing down my back. "Try Commander Tho," I suggested. The major cranked again. This worked. The major chatted with Tho for what seemed to me fifteen minutes--it was probably two minutes. The major hung up the phone, looked at me with a smile and said, "It is okay." He turned and spoke to the lieutenant in Vietnamese. The lieutenant saluted, turned and beckoned to Thinh and me to follow him. I thanked the major and offered him my hand which he took. "It is okay," he repeated. I followed the lieutenant and Sgt Thinh back to the jeep.

As we turned onto the beach I could see that the number of squatting figures on the beach had grown. There were now about eight hundred.

Thinh and I let them know that all was now okay. Eyes that had been fear-filled brightened and smiles broke out on their faces. House Seven was quietly joyful now.

The lieutenant went down the beach to his troops and directed them to move away from the bow door of the LSU. I directed the eight hundred to proceed down the beach and onto the landing ship. I wanted get all those on the beach into the LSU. It took some pushing and pulling but they all got aboard. There was no room to spare. When I saw that all were aboard I pushed my way into the mass. I could not get beyond the bow door area. I found a little space in a gun well at one side of the bow door and I climbed in and settled down for the ride.

The landing ship pulled itself off the beach and headed out to sea. I looked back at Phu Quoc island and could just see the next convoy of trucks pulling onto the beach. Moments later I was able to see the flickering lamps of An Thoi as we sailed past the village.

The sea was fairly calm. The sky was clear and the stars were bright. My light windbreaker was adequate protection from the light sea breeze. After about ten minutes into the voyage I could make out the lights of a ship standing at some distance directly ahead of us. This would be the American Challenger. I pointed it out to some of my Vietnamese colleagues who were in position to see over the bow.

About twenty minutes into our passage, as I sat in the gun well trying to identify constellations, there was some shuffling in the mass of people on the deck below me. A Vietnamese seaman made his way through the packed humanity to get near me and to beckon me to come to the bridge. I thought to myself, "What now?" The incident on the beach had left behind some continuing apprehension in my mind. Murphy's Law again?

Getting to the bridge would take some doing. I was at the bow and the bridge was almost all the way to the stern. I pushed my way through the House Seven throng and climbed up to the bridge. One of the ship's officers thrust an electronic loudhailer into my hand and said, "Captain Thien." Then he pointed off the starboard side of the ship where I could just barely make out the shape of a small vessel. Then I heard Captain Thien's voice coming across the water.

"Mr. T, is it going well?"

I assured him all was well with us and going according to plan. I asked, "What can I do for you, Captain?" He wanted reassurance from me that it would be all right to send his wife and his two children along with us to the American Challenger. I told him we would be more than happy to take his family. The captain then spoke with the LSU skipper. Our vessel slowed and I saw the patrol boat come alongside smoothly, and while the two craft were held side-by-side, three people made the transfer and were safely on board. Captain Thien's craft then turned away, picked up speed and disappeared into the night. I greeted Mrs Thien and the children and the LSU's crew found a place for them in the captain's cabin for the rest of the trip.

Twenty minutes later we were along side the American Challenger. A steep stairway extended down the side of the ship ending at a platform just above the level of the sea. The LSU crew lowered the bow ramp to horizontal position. The idea then was to bring the bow ramp alongside the landing platform. The sea was slightly choppy now and tying up to the landing took a little maneuvering. In charge of the landing operation was the husky, dark curly haired first officer Kukeas, who demonstrated amazing strength and skill. He used himself as a human hawser. He placed himself with one foot on the landing and the other on the bow ramp of the LSU, with one hand grasping a line on the landing and the other holding onto the rail of the LSU. He seemed able to hold the two vessels together against the pull of the choppy seas until his crew were able to complete the tie up. The LSU skipper played his part well also and soon we were in position to start our people up the stairway.

The LSU was bouncing somewhat and I had to step quickly when the landing and the LSU bow ramp were about level. At the top of the stairway a US Marine Corps captain and several enlisted men blocked the way. The captain said, "Welcome aboard." Then he said, "I am sorry, sir, but we will have to search you and your bags." That was fine by me. I remembered the tales of the Danang evacuation. One of the EM patted me down while another went through the two bags I had dropped on the deck beside me. The patdown produced the Colt 38 Police Special which I had strapped at my waist, under my shirt. The marine took the pistol and handed it to his mate who wrote in a small notebook, then placed the gun in a box on deck. I asked if I might have it back later. The answer came from the captain: "No. Sorry, sir, our orders are to confiscate all weapons and dispose of them." There went my souvenir. I would have to leave that bit of the Vietnam experience behind.

Commander Tho came right behind me with his wife and several children and Captain Thien's family. After they and their bags had been searched I took them aside and got the marine captain's permission for them to stay near the entry until could talk with Captain Boucher. It was my intention to try to find some sort of quarters for these principal players in our successful evacuation effort.

I waited a few minutes to see if there was anything I could do at this point. The marines had the situation well in hand. With a helping hand from the Challenger crewmen on the platform the House Seven people were making the quick step from the bouncing LSU ramp onto the ship's landing platform, then up the stairway to the marine processing point on the deck. After the marine search they were directed to go to the forward deck and find a place for the voyage. Sgt. Thinh was one of the first up the stairway. I asked him to stand by the processing point to interpret for the marines as needed. The marine captain welcomed the assistance.

With things going smoothly embarking my people, I went to the bridge to report to Captain Boucher. I told him all had gone well so far, except for the brief hitch on the beach. I said I had brought about 800 of our embassy local employees with me and that my colleagues would follow with about 500 more as soon as the LSU could make the round trip to the beach and back. The captain offered me some coffee which I accepted gratefully. He then took me one deck below the bridge and showed me a small cabin with three bunks and said my colleagues and I could use this space. I pointed out that there were four American officials altogether. He said the fourth member could bunk with the marine captain who had an empty bed in his cabin.

We went back to the bridge. I asked Captain Boucher if we could find a cabin for Commander Tho and his and Captain Thien's families. I explained how they had been critical to our exit from Vietnam and that I would like to do them a favor. The captain said there just was no space he could offer. He suggested I advise Commander Tho to take the two families as far forward as possible on the cargo deck where he could find a more sheltered section of the deck. That was the best he had to offer.

I went back to the processing point and passed on the advice to Commander Tho. I went with him and the two families and got them settled at the base of one of the cargo cranes. They assured me they could manage fine. I went back to the processing point. The House Seven people were slowly climbing the stairway. The older people--the mothers and fathers many of our staffers brought along to keep their families intact--had some difficulty with the new experience of climbing a bouncing stairway. Parents had to pay special attention to the many small children in getting them safely up the steep stairway. The search at the top of the stairway was another new and bewildering experience. After the search they moved quickly toward the forward deck to find choice spaces for the journey to come.

I hung around the processing point for several minutes greeting those I knew well. I soon found there was no need for me at the processing point. Sgt Thinh was all the help the marines needed at that point. After telling the marine officer where he could find me I went up to the bridge. I got another cup of Captain Boucher's good strong coffee and went out on the flying bridge, where I had a bird's eye view of the loading operation. It took a good two hours to get all the people off the bouncing LSU, across the water gap between the two vessels, up the stairs, through the search procedure and onto the freighter's forward deck.

The LSU pulled away from the American Challenger at about two o'clock. It was now the morning of April 30th.

The steel deck of a freighter does not make an especially comfortable seat and surely not a restful bed. Our Vietnamese had been allowed only one small "carry on" bag. If they brought a sweater or coat, they had some cushioning to place between them and the deck. Lucky early arrivals found more luxurious space on wooden hold covers. Always resourceful, some found pieces of cardboard boxes in the ship's trash which they used to soften the steel deck.

In fact, however, our Vietnamese colleagues were little worried about hard beds. Many had known nothing but hard beds their whole lives. They could put up with a lot of hardship, especially at this point in their lives. Sgt Thinh expressed the feeling of most House Seven people. He said, "We consider this no hardship at all. This is just the price we must pay to escape a way of life we do not accept--the Hanoi way."

Further, while we had made no promises, our Vietnamese friends knew that chances were good they would end up in the United States to start a new life in what many of them considered the land of milk and honey. On the other hand, some were not especially happy to leave their homeland. Ms Han, one of our scriptwriters who had come along without any family members, told me of the sadness at having to leave her parents behind. They were older and did not want to leave their village life. While most House Seven staffers had brought their immediate families with them, still they knew they were leaving behind a way of life that was familiar, predictable, and in many ways satisfying. They knew they were headed for a different kind of life, a life with many uncertainties.

A few days into our voyage, chatting with some of the House Seven people, I told them they were having the same experience our American forefathers had gone through in the seventeenth and eighteenth centuries. The Pilgrims particularly. They too fled an unfriendly political environment in the old world. The wooden ships that carried them to the new world may have offered better beds but were probably as crowded as the American Challenger. The Mayflower was surely not as stable and safe as the 20,000 ton freighter. We all got a good laugh out of my history lesson cum morality tale.

After I watched the LSU disappear into the night fatigue began to creep up on me. I had not sat down since I boarded the ship. I lay down on a bench on the boat deck and closed my eyes. I told myself I would rest for just a moment. When I awakened I bolted upright. I had not intended to go to sleep. I looked at my watch; it was four fifteen. Had the evacuation gone on effectively without me? Did any one know what to do without my guidance? Apparently so. I climbed back up to the flying bridge and looked over the foredeck, now well covered with bodies. Most of our people had done what I did, they lay down and were now sleeping after an long tense day and night.

I looked toward the island. No boat lights coming toward the Challenger yet. I had not expected the LSU to return much earlier than five o'clock. I raided Captain Boucher's coffee pot again and sat down to wait for my colleagues and the remainder of our Vietnamese friends.

Five o'clock came and no landing ship. The eastern sky began to show where the sun would appear. Six o'clock came, then seven then eight and still no boat. I began to worry. I talked with the officer on watch on the bridge and we found we had no way to communicate with my colleagues on the beach. Nothing to do but sweat it out.

Captain Boucher appeared and invited me to have some breakfast in the officer's mess. I got the works: eggs, bacon, toast, jam, orange juice, coffee. I returned to my favorite observation spot, the flying bridge and watched nervously for my colleagues.

Around nine o'clock I noticed several small boats approaching the ship. Some of these were little larger than a canoe, others were almost the size of a small landing craft. All were loaded with people, some so overloaded that they were on the verge of swamping. One by one they approached the ships landing platform and begged to come aboard. Captain Boucher came to me and asked if the small boats contained any of our people. I could see no one I recognized on the boats and told the captain they were not our people. Captain Boucher's crewmen on the landing platform began waving the small boats off. The boats would then pull away from the American Challenger and stand off several hundred yards, waiting, hoping for a change of mind by the Americans. This became a continuing process as more small craft came out from the shore and sought permission to come aboard. Later we would learn that many of the people on the small boats were well acquainted with the American Challenger; they were refugees from the refugee camp just north of the Camp Seven. Many of these people had already been through the evacuation. The had been transported from Da Nang, Nha Trang, Vung Tao, and Saigon. Many had debarked from the American Challenger just two days earlier. Some of these had to be forced off the ship. Captain Boucher had no orders to take the refugees further. The small boats waited and hoped as other craft continued to join the circling flotilla standing off the shore side of the freighter.

As the morning dragged on I became increasingly concerned about my colleagues. I suggested to Captain Boucher that I might go ashore in one of his boats to check on them. He suggested patience. He was also reluctant to send a boat and men into an unknown situation. I did not press the point but told myself I would have to do something to ascertain their situation before too much longer. Fortunately further action was not necessary.

Just before ten o'clock the LSU finally appeared in the distance headed for the American Challenger. As the vessel drew closer I could recognize Sam and Bob standing by the wheel house. They waved and Sam gave a thumbs up sign. The sea was quite calm and the landing and LSU tie-up was quickly accomplished. Sam and Bob came up the stairway, all smiles but looking exhausted. They had a story to tell. They had run into the same hold up on the beach that I had gone through. Again Captain Thien could not be found to authorize the transportation of the House Seven staff from the beach to the ship. Why reauthorization was necessary after I had straightened that out the evening before was a mystery. I was able to tell them why they could not locate Thien--he was at sea in pursuit of the LSU to place his family on board to join the evacuation.

I asked where Joe was. Sam said he was bringing the House Seven baggage in a small landing craft and would be along shortly.

The remaining House Seven staffers and their families, about 500 people, were slowly making their way up the stairway, going through the marine corps search and filing forward to find deck space. I took Sam and Bob to meet Captain Boucher and tell their story. Sam explained that Joe would be along soon with the House Seven baggage, then we would be all accounted for.

Joe did not reach the ship until 2 o'clock in the afternoon. He too had a story. He had taken several navy trucks back to the Camp Seven to pick up the bags we had assembled for later transport. He was too late. The refugees from the big camp, after curfew ended at six, had found the House Seven camp deserted and a rich treasure of personal baggage to plunder. They promptly did so.

Don enlivened his story further. As his landing craft pulled away from the beach it came under sniper fire from the shore. He could not determine who was firing at the boat and he and the navy crew got away as fast as they could and headed for the Challenger.

Loss of their bags was a blow to the House Seven group. Fortunes of war. They took it well. They were happy to be aboard the ship and headed away from trouble.

BOAT PEOPLE

When the last of the House Seven people were on board, Captain Boucher asked me to come to the bridge. He pointed to the growing swarm of boats filled with people begging to be taken on board the Challenger. He asked me what I thought he should do. We talked about the American obligation, if any, to help these people. I observed that the United States government played a crucial role in bringing Vietnam to the present sorry pass and that we had helped to instill in these people deep fear of communism. We had encouraged them to run from the communists, we had even made available this ship and many others to help them escape the advancing communist forces. I said there is no place for them to run now. We have done all we can do. Our commitment to the people of Vietnam came to an end on April 28 when we were ordered out of the country. I advised the Captain not to take the boat people pending orders from the Evacuation Command.

Within an hour of our conversation, orders came from the Command: "Take as many refugees as you can carry." The order went down to the landing platform where First Officer Kukeas and his crew signaled to the fleet of small boats that they would be taken on board the Challenger. Immediately, boats of all sizes, frail canoes, motor launches, fishing boats, rafts rushed the landing platform, fighting each other to come along side and discharge their passengers. The American Challenger crew struggled to bring order out of the chaos in the water around them. The transfers from the small boats to the landing were frequently precarious. In the course of the afternoon several people did go into the water but all were pulled out and no one was seriously hurt in the operation.

The marines carried out their mission at the top of the stairway, carefully searching all who boarded, confiscating weapons, recording names and distributing the flow of refugees to the after deck. House Seven had pretty much filled up the forward deck space.

The Challenger continued to load refugees from the boats until dark. Approximately 2000 refugees were finally loaded before the ship got under way about midnight.

A freighter is designed to carry freight not people. But the American Challenger had been modified with a few planks to serve as a passenger ship, so long as the passengers are satisfied with a cold steel deck to sit upon and to sleep on. Sitting and sleeping are the least of a freighter's worries when it comes to carrying people. Natural functions present a problem of serious proportions. The only toilets are in the officer and crew quarters, and only have sufficient capacity for those who work the ship. This is where the planks came into play. The ship's carpenters had constructed creatively designed privies that extended over the port and starboard sides of the ship, two eight-holers forward and two aft. Each pot was walled off from the next, affording a minimum of privacy, more for short than tall people. It took a little courage to mount one of these facilities, precariously balanced over the side with nothing but space and the sea below. Necessity managed to make the facilities work to the relative satisfaction of the clientele and spared the ship from natural disasters.

Water was another critical consideration for the deck-loaded passengers. Fresh water for drinking was provided by a number of Lister Bags (military-style water containers) placed around the deck. Drinking water would be in tight supply and the passengers were allowed two cups in the morning and two in the afternoon. Hoses supplying seawater for washing were available to the passengers at several points on deck. This was rationed only by the necessity to allow everyone a chance to get at the hose in turn.

The US Marine Corps ran a first class mess (freighter deck class) for the refugees on the American Challenger. The marines had placed several huge kettles on deck, forward and aft. Heated by steam hoses from the ship's boilers, the kettles were loaded with rice and vegetables and some C-ration meat. The cooking process and the feeding went throughout the daylight hours in order to provide one hot meal per day for each refugee. The marines recruited refugees to actually do the cooking, dishing up, clean up and other mess duties. These jobs were actually much sought after--access to food is a great motivator. The marines came prepared with a meal ticket system. Each person was provided a meal ticket which was punched when he received his bowl of congee. Our cruise passengers were a little hungry much of the time, one bowl of rice and vegetable was not much, but they were far from starvation. The marine mess which made the voyage supportable for the refugees was only one of the outstanding services provided by the USMC.

MARINES

The seventy men of "November" detachment, the marine security force assigned to the American Challenger, came from the Third Service Battalion of the Third Marine Division on Okinawa. Led by Captain Mike Mallick, most were veterans of the Vietnam War. Two of the marines were Vietnamese speakers from the division's intelligence staff. A five-man team of US Navy medical corpsmen came with "November." The job of the marines was to provide security on board the ship and to assist with the management of the mass of refugees taken aboard. No task was outside the job description of "November" detachment.

Captain Mallick's troops were in charge of the Challenger's deck where they managed a refugee city of five thousand people. They organized a workforce from the refugee population to accomplish the massive job of feeding everyone and keeping the deck clean, orderly, and as livable as possible.

As one of their most important functions, the navy corpsmen established a hospital in one corner of the boat deck--one deck up from where the masses were lodged. They recruited three medical doctors from the refugees and assembled a corps of experienced nurses to assist them. They had a supply of bandages, commonly used medicines, and medical instruments. The hospital was busy throughout the voyage. I never looked in on the outdoor sickbay that there was not activity. Minor cuts and bruises were routine. Seasickness pills were handed out as long as supplies were available. A popular item. More serious illnesses were treated as best the corpsmen and doctors could manage and were placed in a holding patter until we could land and turn them over to more complete medical facilities. Two babies were born during the voyage, one on the first day at sea, a second en route from the Philippines to Guam. Two new US citizens.

USS DUBUQUE

The American Challenger spent the afternoon of 30 April taking on board refugees from the swarm of small boats that continued to stream out from Phu Quoc Island. Suddenly, about three o'clock, I heard Captain Ma1lick shout for every one on deck to get down or take cover inside or on the port side of the ship. I ducked into a passageway on the boat deck and peeked out to try to see what was going on. The marines dropped their refugee management duties, grabbed up their M-16s, and took prone firing positions on the deck, aiming their rifles off the starboard side of the ship. I saw the marine officer point toward the land. I looked where he was pointing and saw a flotilla of four Vietnamese Navy vessels steaming toward us. The largest was the size of a coast guard cutter, the others were smaller patrol craft. Captain Mallick, not knowing what the intentions of these warships might be toward us, was not taking any chances. Had the Vietnamese Navy ships been taken over by Vietcong cadre? Had disaffected South Vietnamese forces decided to take a prize to turn over to the Hanoi government?

Unknown to us on the Challenger, the US Navy had the same concerns. We did not know the US Navy was anywhere near Phu Quoc island. But suddenly they were there. The USS Dubuque, an 8600 ton amphibious transport dock, with a destroyer escort hove into sight about three miles to the west, off the starboard bow of the Challenger. The Dubuque radioed that they were moving to provide protection for the Challenger. The destroyer turned and headed toward the Challenger.

Now we looked back at the supposed threatening Vietnamese warships. They were now quite close and it quickly became apparent they had no hostile intensions. We could see women and children on the decks of the vessels. Deck guns were covered and not manned. All waved in a most friendly manner toward us. They did not seek to come aboard the Challenger. They would take care of themselves. The four little ships sailed right on by us and out to sea. They were headed for Thailand, Malaysia, The Philippines, anywhere they could land. The South Vietnamese Navy had joined the evacuation.

The US Navy destroyer turned back and rejoined the Dubuque standing further out at sea. They would escort the Challenger out of Vietnamese waters later in the day.

MAY FIRST

The Challenger got under way about one in the morning on May 1. Captain Boucher had been ordered to suspend taking on refugees and to leave Vietnam territorial waters. Boats continued to approach the American Challenger seeking refuge as the vessel put out to sea. Many of the frail craft continued to follow in the wake of the large freighter, falling further and further behind until they disappeared in the night.

It was clear and sunny when I awakened on May 1 and the South China Sea was very calm as the American Challenger followed a course around the Ca Mau Peninsula (The Delta) and then northeast to rendezvous with the evacuation fleet off Vung Tao.

After breakfast in the officers dining room, Sam, Joe, Bob and I went down to the cargo decks to check on the House Seven people. A few were seasick, and others would become so, but all were in good spirits and making the best of the situation. We told them it would only be about three days to Subic Bay in the Philippines and the tough part would be over. We would have to revise that story later.

About eight o'clock we steamed past Con Son Island, site of the Saigon government's political prison camps and the infamous tiger cages in which particularly recalcitrant Vietcong were held until they promised to improve their behavior or were disposed of in some officially or unofficially prescribed manner.

All during the morning small boats coming from the Delta, over the horizon to the west, approached the Challenger seeking to be rescued from the unknown fate overtaking their country. The ship's orders did not permit stopping to pick up the boat people and she continued on to the evacuation fleet rendezvous, about sixty miles southeast of Vung Tao in the South China Sea.

We arrived at the rendezvous just before noon to join an impressive gathering of vessels of many types and sizes. I spotted at least two aircraft carriers. There were several landing ship docks, a cruiser, several destroyers and other US Navy ships. A half dozen freighters were among the ships anchored in the choppy waters. Several helicopters shuttled among the ships continually during the day. Headquarters for the evacuation fleet was the amphibious command ship USS Blue Ridge (LCC 19).

The American Challenger dropped anchor about one mile from the Blue Ridge. I requested Captain Boucher's permission to communicate with our superiors who were on the Blue Ridge. We got the deputy chief of station on line and reported that all the American staff and all the House Seven people were safely on board. The deputy gave us a "well done." He invited us to join him on the Blue Ridge. We conferred among ourselves and decided we would remain on board the American Challenger and complete the adventure with the House Seven staff. We asked that our families be notified that we were safe and would rejoin them as soon as possible.

The command asked Captain Boucher to take on 4000 additional refugees from the Grenville Victory, another evacuation freighter, which was badly overloaded. The transferring of refugees began about one o'clock and continued all day and into the night. The Challenger also took on food and other stores, enough for seven days, according to the ship's first officer.

The refugees from the Grenville Victory appeared to be mostly poor Vietnamese peasants and fishermen. There were many rather ragged little children and babies. There was also a good number of younger men who probably had been soldiers.

The scene at the rendezvous was one of frenzied activity. Small boats arrived throughout the day from the Vietnam mainland. They maneuvered to come along side the evacuation vessels to be taken aboard. There was a lot of crowding and pushing, and the marines and the merchant seamen had to be rough to make them queue up and wait their turn. Many of the small craft, in danger of sinking under the masses of people crowded on their decks, did not look as though they could wait their turn. Many of the boats looked like they had been dug out of the mud and pressed into service for this one-way voyage. The boats were simply cast adrift after they unloaded onto one of the evacuation ships.

One of the most amazing seagoing craft among the fleeing vessels was a huge barge which must have been a hundred yards long and possibly fifteen yards wide. Towed by a tug, every inch of space was occupied by refugees. They were fortunate that the sea was not any choppier than it was; I am certain many would have fallen overboard in heavier seas. The refugees were taken off the barge in small landing craft which then transported them to one of the landing ship docks (LSD) in an amazing operation. The landing craft entered the LSD at the stern, disappearing inside the huge vessel, where they unloaded in sheltered waters.

The American Challenger continued to take on refugees and supplies until about two thirty on the morning of May 2, then sailed for Subic Bay in The Philippines where our Vietnamese passengers were to be placed in refugee camps. We steamed in convoy with three other refugee-loaded freighters, escorted by two US Navy destroyers. Both May 2 and 3 were fine days and the seas were smooth which made life more bearable for the massed refugees on those steel decks.

In the morning on May 2 we learned from radio news casts about the American flight from Saigon: the helicopters from the roof of the embassy, communist tanks in the presidential palace, the capitulation of all South Vietnamese forces, Saigon renamed Ho Chi Minh City. It was all over for Vietnam as we knew it.

At 7 AM on May 3 a second baby was born in the makeshift hospital on the boat deck of the American Challenger. Mother and baby were fine. In the afternoon we were disappointed to learn that the refugees camps at Subic Bay were filled to capacity and we would have to sail three more days, to Guam.

On May 4 we steamed through the Zamboanga Straits, with lush green Philippine islands on both sides and to the north several cone-shaped volcanoes. The good weather continued through the remainder of the voyage, sparing our shelter-less passengers more misery.

We docked at the Long Pier at Agana, Guam about midnight on May 6. My colleagues and I were not able to leave the ship until after 5 AM on the 7th when the last of our people were in the refugee processing system. We took a cab to the Cliff Hotel and collapsed into our beds.

An Agency team sent from headquarters assumed responsibility for handling the processing of the House Seven people. Sam and Bob remained in Guam to assist the headquarters team. Joe departed immediately for Canada, home. I received orders to proceed on to Taipei, Taiwan, where Lois was living in safe-haven quarters. Taipei Station had an operational job they wanted me to undertake.